Ask Me ....,
Stood Here

A Bristol Channel Swim Tale

Alec Richardson

An ordinary man swimming across an extraordinary
body of water.

Image Credits:

Swimmer (Title page):   Jake Richardson

Approaching the Slipway (Chapter 5):   Jake Richardson

All other images and cover photography: Alec Richardson

To

Jo, Jake, Stan and Eddie

Thank you for tolerating the things I do

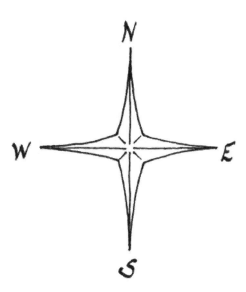

Table of Contents

Foreword

Wednesday 16th August started with a 3am alarm in order to get Mr Richardson to Portishead Marina before 5am. This was with the purpose of him fulfilling his dream of swimming The Bristol Channel from Penarth to Clevedon, even though there are perfectly good roads which connect the two.

And, indeed, the dream was duly fulfilled in the very impressive time of 5 hours and 58 minutes. Well done to Alec and his team for the not insignificant planning and preparation which has gone into making this happen. I cannot express how reassuring it was as I left the Marina this morning to know that he was being looked after by Steve Price, Laura Nesbitt, Gavin Oliver and our own Jake Richardson and not forgetting skipper Paul Wells and Ruby D without whom it wouldn't have been possible. Huge thanks to all of the above and to the people who turned up at Clevedon Beach a full hour earlier than planned after things went more swimmingly than anticipated!

I'm so glad that all the planning has been worth it, congratulations to Alec on a fantastic achievement and in the words of my Uncle Rick, don't do any more stupid things now!! Or at least not for a while! Please!

Joanna Richardson

A Few Basic Facts

Date: Wednesday 16th August 2017

Route: Penarth Slipway to Clevedon Slipway

Distance: 13 miles direct, 15.3 miles actual path on the day (tide did some of the work though!)

Start Time: 6:30 am

Swim Time: 5 hours, 58 minutes and 03 seconds

Tide Conditions: Tidal coefficient 60, just coming off a neap tide. Overall height variation approx. 7.20m

Low Water: 07:38, 3.2m

High Water: 13:57, 10.4m

Weather Conditions: Wind average force 2 to 3, southerly moving to south-easterly, gusts strengthening through the day. Cloudy with sunny spells. Air temperature rising from 10 to 16 degrees through the morning.

Water Temperature: 16 degrees Celsius

ASK ME WHY I'M STOOD HERE

M y lake swims are a little bit shorter now than they used to be. Scampering over to Clevedon between the dad-taxi runs was once about maximising time in the water, but now I seem to be sacrificing a length or two to stand on the rocks and stare out across the sea. Its brawn and tone are different every time, as is the ensuing flow of musings in my head. Much of it swirls above an undercurrent of satisfaction, but it is mostly a mess of wonderings and fleeting, uncatchable emotions. Any passer-by who might see me standing, and staring, could well wonder what it is that absorbs me….. perhaps I should get a t-shirt with 'ask me why I'm stood here' printed on the back. This book is the answer to that question.

Of course, I want to talk about my swim, my preparation, my experience, my developing thoughts. Some of my local swimming community may already have noticed that. It's just that I think I prefer it if I'm not the one to bring it up. My swim-lines have crossed with many people who have outstanding stories of tough and gritty challenges both past and future and, without exception, they are wholly unconcerned and unaffected by the enormity of their exploits. Consequently, alongside every surge of enthusiasm as I talk (or write) about my swim comes an equally vigorous rush of embarrassment.

I am under no illusion that this was the greatest swim ever. For a bit of perspective, I have recently read Sean Conway's "Hell and High Water" so in comparison I don't think that a designation of 'epic' could be bestowed on my adventure which finished on the beach, at lunchtime, with a sandwich and a mug of tea. Nonetheless, on top of the six hours of swimming in lively tidal water, add in the level of preparation and planning required to ensure the specific start and finish points on either side of such an awkward stretch of water, and I do think it's fair to claim that this was a significant and interesting challenge. There are many, many inspirational swimmers whose stories are there for us to read, or whose uplifting speeches can be found recorded for us to absorb. Swims of enormity, channels of terror and temperatures of extremes. All conquered with character of huge strength, determination of godly proportion and extreme adjustments to lifestyle. Enthralling and wildly inspirational, but so far removed from where most of us are that their words may strike a massive gong in our hearts, but do not give us the tools to find a challenge on our own scale or show us the first small step. I hope to sneak into that gap with this account. I am just a fairly ordinary bloke who fancied doing something a little out of the ordinary. I was in no position to give up my job and I did not want to commit to anything which uncomfortably squeezed time with my

2

family. My financial resources are limited, travel and remote accommodation are expensive. Mostly, I wanted it to be part of what I already do, where I already am, who I am already with: an extension of me, not an alternative reality. I think this is what most of us want when we are looking to challenge ourselves, so I really hope that this account entertains, but gives you plenty to think about. Lots and lots of little things which add up to something substantial. What small things could you start doing now to begin widening your view and open up enticingly realistic dreams of something special, something yours?

I could have tracked and shared my progress as it was ongoing, but blogging holds no appeal for me. I trundle through my days wading about in treacle-like mundanity; to churn all that out would have been no more than careless squandering of the bits and bytes of our modern cloud. So I have waited until it is done, I have had time to reflect and now, with this swim as the theme, I am excited about gathering words with which to crochet little paragraphs to knit together, hopefully creating a warm and cosy blanket worthy of a few moments curled up on the sofa, reading specs on, glass in hand.

My swim was not a carefully controlled experiment and this account is not a rigorously researched and referenced scientific report. I am not claiming factual accuracy and expertise beyond that of the experience of the swim itself and my understanding of the knowledge of those who were generous enough to assist me. I researched enough to be able to execute the swim, and that was it. Much of what appears from here on is descriptive. A sharing of the experience, my observations and my interpretations. I just hope you enjoy it and, maybe, get something of use from it. Feel free to disagree with what I say, there are plenty of people who know considerably more about long distance sea swimming, the Bristol Channel and the

3

Severn Estuary than I do. You may be one of them. I stand by my mermaid fact though.

I suspect it may become swiftly apparent, but I would like to point out at this early stage that I am not a writer. I am a mathematics teacher with an engineering background. Words for me are solid, tangible things to be bolted, glued and interlocked to create some larger, linear structure with a simple concrete form, meaning and purpose; no pieces missing or left-over. If my use or misuse of punctuation, grammar or sentence structure offends your better-educated sensibilities, then I apologise; feel free to tut your way through. In re-reads of my descriptions I can see that they are frequently cumbersome with detail, claustrophobic with repetition, narrowing your vision until you are left with little choice but to see things in a particular way. How I would love to just scatter gentle hints and let your imagination do the rest. It doesn't happen, I am not confident enough; can't take the risk. Should you have to re-read the occasional badly formed, gallumphing sentence to extract its meaning, I truly hope it turns out to be worth the effort. As I write I realise I have a tendency to overdramatise slightly: not much and not all of the time, but definitely when it's important to me that I give you every possible chance to catch my drift. I spy myself taking a point and repeating it threefold using increasingly desperate tricks to convey meaning, clarify the essence. My prose seems to be the bit of the rollercoaster where the gears clank noisily into place beneath the train, juddering you up the slope to gain the necessary height. The quality of the resulting ride (hopefully more rewarding than sickening) may well depend as much on your own patience and tolerance as on the certainty of gravity itself. Point laboured? Twenty-one years of trying to deviously sow the seeds of, instil and then drive home, "do not add the denominators!" is probably to blame.

Two strands have emerged, separate but dependent on each other. Firstly, there is the story: how I arrived at this swim, the execution of the swim itself, and where the experience has left me now. Secondly, there is some guidance to this commingling of Severn and sea and what is involved in swimming here, maybe even crossing it. I cannot tell one tale without the other. I offer no history, no study of the flora and fauna, no social comment and a slightly embarrassing lack of interest in anything I did not need to swot up on to complete the swim. I have contemplated digging a little deeper into the history of Bristol Channel swimmers but put it swiftly aside as I realised trying to include it would likely just condemn this to the ne'er to be finished pile. The guidance I have scattered within is a summary of how and what I have learned, my understanding of the channel: some of it gained before contemplating the crossing, much of it because of that contemplation. I managed the swim largely because of this accumulated knowledge and drew on it both in the preparation and on my way across. Sometimes the two strands weave seamlessly, else while the loom becomes clogged and tangled as one strand runs faster than the other. I've done my best; a few snags, loops and bleeds in the pattern but a warm cloak nonetheless – for a walk in the dark.

Some basic and not especially meticulous research (that's the best you're going to get) has led me to understand that Penarth and Clevedon are both on the coast of the Severn Estuary (or Mouth of the Severn), and to be in the Bristol Channel proper I would need to be south of the line between Lavernock Point and Sand Point. If I'd been a little slower or left Penarth a little longer before the turn of the tide, I may have been swept across this boundary, but it turns out I only tracked within 500m of it, staying in the waters of the Severn Estuary. As the moniker of a feral, fast-moving stretch of water "The Bristol Channel" is the Yorkie Bar to the Milk Chocolate Button of "The Severn

Estuary". Don't get me wrong, the Estuary is potentially brutal, even further up where it is only a couple of miles across, but I fear that the word "estuary" does not conjure the correct image for most. Resultingly, I generally tell myself and everyone else that I swam across The Bristol Channel. Anyway, the water I dragged myself through that day had only just charged in from the channel to get to where I was.

Much like keeping your outdoor swims going to the middle of winter, if you've made it this far there is a good chance you've got the gumption to manage the rest, so I should probably shut up and let you get on with it. Enjoy.

The British Long Distance Swimming Association

Bristol Channel

The President and Executive Committee
have pleasure in awarding this certificate to

Alec Richardson

who completed the course from

Penarth   to   *Clevedon*

on   *16ᵗʰ August 2017*

in   *5*   hours   *58*   minutes   *3*   seconds

President

Recorder

12.7 miles

7

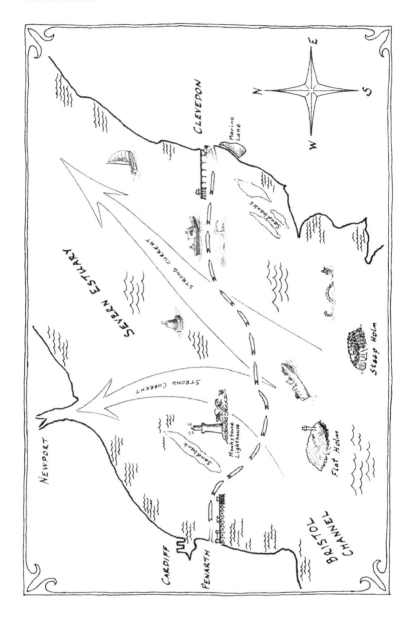

Chapter 1

IT'S JUST A (SMALLER) CHANNEL CROSSING – SO WHAT?

This channel, this transition from brackish estuary to rampant sea, is a little different to many others which attract traversing swimmers; it is a funnel; with a cork in the end. The resulting tidal range causes general flows of up to 7mph and the surface of the water to rise and fall over 14 metres on spring tides; that puts it in the top three highest tidal ranges in the world. To complicate matters further the channel bed is very confused about its identity and likes to get in on the action. It is not deep below the surface, allowing the water to flow relatively evenly and predictably above it; it interacts and jostles for position with the surface of the water as it rises and falls, thus creating an ever-changing mish-mash of localised flow patterns within the overall rush up and down the channel. There are swathing, hungry mudflats frilling the edges, expansive sandbanks exposed at low water and narrow, 20-metre-deep channels taking huge cargo ships to Avonmouth and Newport. Get caught in the flow of the Newport bound one and dreams of determining your own landing point will dissolve quickly. This variation in terrain for the waters to flow around and over creates rapidly changing currents which are nigh on impossible to chart. A fast, linear flow across the top of a sandbank can suddenly turn through surprising angles as the falling tide causes the water to flow off the sides of it. Currents flowing either side of a sandbank (exposed, or maybe hidden in the few metres below the inscrutable surface) re-join at the far end in a swirling mess of eddies which would spin a swimmer one way then the other like a fairground waltzer, then spit them out 100 metres further upstream with lungs full of silt. The difference in flow as you cross from shallow mudflats to the edge of deeper channels can roll you over, turn you round and spank you on the backside in the space of three strokes. All of this, combined with wind effects, contributes to possibly subtle, but always significant, variation in wave magnitude and direction at the surface itself. The proximity of land and narrowing of the channel causes the wind to barrel about excitedly, its desire to switch locally from onshore breezes to offshore breezes following sunrise and sunset conflicting with the prevailing woosh of the day. The resulting air patterns conspire with the currents to fabricate a capricious rollercoaster for the swimmer. What looks like a steady few hundred yards of four-foot waves will most likely cycle between Gromit-like sections of helpful, regular and surf-able slopes, followed by well-meaning but haphazard Wallace-like bulges, then into a bouncy, over-excited bunny of irregular, rhythm-spoiling peaks and troughs and finally metamorphose into a monstrous were-rabbit of gnarly, back-biting breakers that slap your recovering arm back into the water and squirt coarse jets of seawater under the seal of your goggles. And when I say seawater I'm not talking about that clear blue-green-grey stuff which surrounds most of Britain; this water is brown and too silty to see through, cooled and filled with debris by rivers and rife with invisible creatures gritty, gutsy and gruff enough to handle the terrain. The local mermaids, though apparently friendly, have beards coarse enough to scour a hull clean. There are thornback ray, treacherous tope, ferocious flounder and cadaverous conger; fortunately, the carnivorous cod are a winter fish. If you are an outdoor swimmer and have never watched Jeremy Wade's River Monsters, keep it that way. Jelly fish make it this far up, I have seen vast carpets of what I think were moon jelly fish along the edge of Portishead Marina, and Portugese Man O' War sightings have been known on North Devon beaches, only a few miles south. In addition to all this at various points along the way there are expanses of craggy rock which loom in and out of view with the tide, islands, a lighthouse or two, some seemingly fast-moving shipping buoys and plenty of floating traffic.

Otherwise, it's just a channel crossing.

Chapter 2

WHY?

"Because it's there. Because you can. Because you're a daft bugger Alec."

Facebook comment from Jeremy Murgatroyd

To be honest, having read Jeremy's quote, you can probably skip the next few hundred words; I'm unlikely to add anything more enlightening than that.

"Mid-life Crisis" is a phrase I am not keen on, but as an answer to "why?" it proves effective. The enquirer usually nods, knowingly, and leaves it at that. Maybe this condition has become so well understood in the modern age that it really is a "nuff said" answer. My suspicion is, however, that we have all learnt not to delve deeper into this particular can of worms. Essentially though, it is the truthful answer in this instance. If you like, jump ahead now as I am about to dissect a couple of the biggest, fattest worms from that aforementioned can.

Right now, somewhere near the middle of my adult life, I am questioning where I have ended up and what is ahead of me. There are two major factors contributing to frequent reconsiderations of my most likely path from here. The first is physical and unique to me, the second is career related and political, and both are major drivers behind my decision to do this swim. Of course, they are not independent of each other;

one is a chicken, the other an egg – and there we have the ingredients of a hearty omelette, and an appropriate cliché.

My youth was intensely physical; swimming, cycling, running, cricket, squash, weights. I never saw a reason for this to change. At the age of twenty-seven I contracted campylobacter food poisoning. It put me in hospital for a week, robbing me of two stone. Combined with the energy drain of being new to teaching and returning to work sooner than was wise it took just three months to exhaust me to the depths of depression. Eventually thinking I'd fought off the food poisoning itself I spent the next ten years being outwardly pathetic. I had frequent bouts of crippling stomach pain, I was almost constantly exhausted. I came down with every bug and virus which came to sit in my classroom. Occasionally I would feel 'well' and attempt some sort of exercise only for it to leave me feeling too feeble to function effectively for the next few days. I missed a lot of work. Much of the time I spent at work I felt awful, and wished I was at home in bed. I lost all confidence in myself professionally, physically and as a husband and father. Ambition was squeezed out by survival. In the absence of any physical diagnosis (possible IBS and peppermint tablets was the best I was offered) I eventually came to believe that everyone felt like this, I was just the only person too weak-willed to cope with it.

In the last weeks of the summer term in 2006, Jo came home to find me in bed curled around a hot water bottle with excruciating stomach pain, again. She rang for an ambulance and, now pumped full of morphine, off I went. I was booked in to theatre to have my appendix removed the following morning, but yet again I fought off the pain and nearly got discharged instead. Fortunately, the senior consultant popped in to check me over and having heard my history suggested he may as well go ahead with the appendectomy if only to eliminate it as a factor (or maybe because he had a surgery quota to hit by the end of the month?). My doctor had recently given up trying to find a diagnosis for my second-rate attempt at being a real man and had referred me to a Gastroenterology specialist. My first appointment came a month or so after my surgery. The gastroenterologist read the toxicology report from my appendix and the decade of notes from my doctor and explained it all very simply. I had been constantly fighting campylobacter food poisoning which had insidiously concealed itself in my appendix all this time. My immune system was so busy with this it couldn't cope with much else. Appendicitis was never diagnosed because the hideous little pocket of nastiness wasn't quite positioned where it should have been. He confidently dismissed me with an open appointment with the caveat that I had a long way to go to get my immune system back to where it should be, but assured me I would not need to see him again. He was right. Another ten years later and I finally feel strong and what I imagine is somewhere near normal. I have most of my physical confidence back. I am still apparently more susceptible than most of those around me to catching bugs, and get hit regularly by migraines. I wouldn't dare argue the case that I have a strong constitution, though I wish it to be so. Overall, however, what I can make my body do is once again under my control. I am still guarded and cautious, but excited about making up for lost time. I have recovered my active mojo and I intend to do gutsy stuff, sweaty stuff, interesting stuff, burly stuff: stuff which matters to me, stuff of my making, stuff my kids will remember. The joy of it is that I don't have to enter events or competitions to do it. It doesn't all have to be big stuff and there is no need for me to do anything better or faster than anyone else. I'm going to do stuff for me, but do my best to drag a few others along for the ride. A challenging swim seems to fit the bill.

During this time of poor health and painfully gradual return to strength I have married, bought a house and set a family in motion. All the major, long-term financial decisions have been made, set in stone, based on the deal I thought I signed up for as a public servant, where loyalty and good will were, eventually, rewarded. Over the past five years the government have presented that reward as an effective pay cut of about 5 percent and an extra 8 years on my working life. A callous and thoughtless rug-pull. Not just for me, but for the profession, for the future education of our children. Unwisely, the additional years have been put at the end of my career when I very much doubt I will be able to cope with the demands of this particular job, even on a part-time basis. I don't have an issue with the need to work beyond 60, but not in the classroom. I now cannot afford to stop at 60, but neither can I wait until then to find alternative income. Each year brings me closer to deciding that the energy and commitment required between now and then is no longer worth the diminishing reward. I have to plan and act now to give me some sort of flexibility in the way I earn and work. The amplitude of the energy demand wave increases year-on-year, the peaks grow higher and broader and as I age, I cannot be sure how much longer I will have the resolve to keep scrabbling up the scree-ridden ascents. A clean break or entire career shift is unlikely, I have the aforementioned long-term commitments to see through, but some sort of change is necessary to give me choices in the future.

I am now a qualified Open Water Swimming Coach. Maybe an additional income stream, maybe just a distraction. Either way, I have a track record, friends I've helped and clients I've worked with who would knock out an honest critique of my work. But we now live in a world of soundbites, headlines and USPs – where carefully placed hints and half-facts can be glossed up to look like credibility. Credentials, prove-able acts, reliable testimony; good, honest credibility - I don't have the balls to operate without it, my conscience would grass on me. Not surprisingly, I am a little sensitive about the "Those who can't do, teach" myth so having tangible evidence that "I can" is important to me. A significant swim ought to take care of that.

......and why this swim?

Penarth to Clevedon isn't just a 13 mile swim. It shares much with, but is hugely distant from 80 or so lengths of Clevedon Marine Lake.

Stroking out 13 miles in the sea does not have to be a big deal. I could simply have headed for Swanage Bay. It is a beautiful stretch of water to swim in. Unlike the Bristol Channel, it is clear - you can gauge your progress watching the rocks, weed, crabs and rippled sand pass beneath you. Unlike the Bristol Channel, it has a double tide of stunted amplitude – there is always swimmable water there. The mile and a half swim along the beach from the pier to Ballard Cliff is one of my favourites. There and back a few times and you've done your time, covered your miles. Maybe with a kayaker for feeds, maybe just have a mate sit in a deck chair for the day and lob you a bottle from the jetty as you go by. Yes, the tidal flow saunters lazily along the beach and back, so if it's a spring tide it will be noticeably harder work at times, but it won't take you off course and the pay-off will come when you turn the other way. Sometimes, the wind deviates from its preferred south-westerly and comes at the land from the east, creating some chop and swell which would be useful to hone your open water skills. If it all gets a bit much? Just swim the 50 yards back to the beach, get out and walk home. Six hours of that may be a decent way to crack a qualifying swim for the English Channel, but as a challenge in planning and logistics it offers little more than looking up the opening times of the local pool and checking the weather.

My 5-mile swim the previous year from Swanage Pier, along the bay, out around Ballard Point to Old Harry Rocks then on to Knoll Beach – that was something bigger, an opening of a door. It encompassed a couple of miles around the cliffs, offering no exit from the water and taking in a wider range of tricky currents and flows. I really enjoyed planning that swim; organised as a thank you to the people responsible for getting me into the life of open water swimming. I relished the slow process of gathering information, checking timings, reading tidal flow charts, co-ordinating land support and booking a table for the post-swim curry; something to work towards during the dark, winter evenings. Even re-igniting my mildly creative embers to draw the certificates, and pinching old swimming medals from my kids to dish out at the end added something surprisingly positive to the event. Five of us swam it, two more on kayaks, and a gaggle of land-based supporters – it was our swim, hook, line and sinker; and so much sweeter for it. We didn't have to read the briefing document when it eventually arrived in our inbox, we wrote it ourselves. Emergency contact details and procedures taking the same priority as café stops. It even gave me excuses to get out and do interesting stuff under the guise of preparation; a glorious paddle along part of the route with my son Stan to test the phone signal at the base of the cliffs was a memorable highlight. I came out of it with new acquaintances and contacts, discovering exceptionally helpful people along the way. Seeking out local knowledge I fired off a few emails with a quick description of my intentions, the opening gambit being "Is this a daft idea?". The local open water swimming club responded to say that it had been passed on to their safety team, but I never heard anything back. In contrast, my biggest boost came from a long chat with Dan who runs "Fore Adventure" based at Studland's Middle Beach. He organises kayaking trips along the very route I wanted to swim, so was well placed to talk me through the timings of the tides and the currents we should be wary of around the tip of the headland. Most importantly, he was hugely encouraging. We even ran into him and a group of his kayakers en-route and I was able to thank him in person from the water. We have shaken hands between waves and kayak a few times since. My phone call to inform the local coastguard came in a close second; I was nervously expecting a tough inquisition, maybe even discouragement, but was met with helpful advice, a genuine thank you for thinking to inform them and a reassurance that the patrol vessel which was usually out at that time would come and check how we were getting on.

That was a cracking weekend, with a great swim in the middle of it. Unkind weather rolled out tough conditions along Swanage Bay and out around the headland; rain, a cold, atypical south-easterly wind and 3-foot swell with regular breakers ambushing us from behind. If it had been a large, paid, organised event I suspect it would have been cancelled, but it was our (correct) decision to go ahead with the swim as we all knew our capabilities and understood the contingencies in place. Some of those came in to play, but as a result we all proudly completed the swim safely - knowing a little more about ourselves and each other.

I am fortunate enough to be able to spend some of my time in that part of Dorset; by no means a local, but familiar. Being there for a walk, with the kids, or out on my bike - I now look at the beach, the cliffs, the chalk stacks, the water in a completely different way. A regular reminder of good times, so much better than a few photographs. Something local, something right here in my sphere of existence, stumbling across a little boost here and there as I go about my business. I came away from this Dorset adventure understanding that choosing the path less travelled resonated strongly with me, far more than buying a ticket for even the most spectacular of well-trodden routes.

One thousand waffley words about a completely different swim when trying to justify my choice of the Bristol Channel? Get to the point, man! (Don't hold your breath). My fondness for the estuary is strongly linked to my lack of fondness of choice (this, again, could fill a few pages if I let it). Choice is held up as an indicator of progress, a champion of self-entitlement, a signpost to freedom. So, so wrong. It is a waster of time, a sapper of energy, a cause of unease and uncertainty, a caster of self-doubt. I long to walk down Nailsea High Street and spot a newly opened Berni Inn; if you don't remember their menu, then off you toddle to do a bit of research. The Bristol Channel doesn't offer choice. You do what it says, and you do it when it says so, or you don't do it at all. You can't find a loophole in the small print, or use your wealth to gain some advantage. If you want to swim in it, you sodding well do as it tells you, and you prepare yourself the same as everyone else. Your chance to swim it isn't steered, restricted by a set of rules or the allocation of a slot. The obstacle course you have to negotiate to get to the start point has not been created by a committee, sub-clause beneath sub-clause burying the joy. These obstacles have been crafted by the elements from the shrapnel of a mighty battle between earth, wind and water.

I didn't want a swim, I wanted a swim-based project, a more substantial version of the one above. Stuff to learn, people to find, friends to make. Research to do; plans to sketch out, revise, dump and re-write. Expansive, nearby views to scan and contemplate, to overlay on charts and schedules. Something local; full-on immersion in my environment, my swim-hood, among my homies. If it's just a step up the ladder and I fancy a longer swim sometime in the future, I can count this as a serious trial run. It encompasses the bulk of the elements of many marathon swims in a more compact, feisty package – more Barry McGuigan than Frank Bruno. Boxes ticked, why look any further?

It has taken some time, now the swim is done, for the full effect to take hold, but it has, and I am content with my decision. One winter having passed since making it across I sit here in just my boxers, on a warm, sunny spring bank holiday, passing the time until I head for the lake for a sunset swim. I am looking forward to enjoying my achievement a little bit more as the sun dips behind the Welsh hills. Arrive as the crowds leave, sluice out a refreshing mid-effort hour, maybe a 1K Individual Medley in there somewhere (the lake is 250m long) without the worry of butterfly-battered shoulders setting back my training. Dry off and crack open that flask. Sip and natter away as the sun teases unexpected colour from the surface of the channel, gently shifting its palette to the sky.

Penarth doesn't look all that far away on a clear evening.

Go on – ask me why I'm stood here.

Chapter 3

PREPARATION

Taking on this swim was not just about the few hours I would spend immersed in the water on the day, but also about using the complete project to encourage myself to engage more effectively with the swimming community; I was aware there was so much more for me to learn about open water swimming, but it wasn't going to happen without a purpose. It was clear from the start I would not make it across the Channel without help during the swim, and also seeking out experience well beforehand to help me manage both the logistics and my training. I am still gratefully embarrassed by the quality and quantity of experience I was able to tap into and surround myself with just from the local community. Clevedon, with its Marine Lake, fascinating sea and concentration of expertise really is a centre of excellence for open water swimming.

Aside from a couple of speculative conversations with two fellow swimmers as to the likely mechanics of organising such a swim, for the first three months or so I had told no one of my intention; a sitting duck armed only with a part-baked idea and a reasonable capacity for coldish open water swimming. This is not like the English Channel where there exists a structure, a governing body, a methodology, well documented experience, bucket-loads of advice and endless blogs. An hour scampering about on the internet and I was pretty clear about what I would need to do if it was the English Channel I had set my sights on, but although that undeniable challenge spoke to me on one level, it wasn't stroking my soul (particularly as it didn't take long to work out the £250 per mile price tag). Contrastingly, every time I swam at Clevedon, lake or sea, I would look across to Wales, scan round to Flat Holm and Steep Holm, bring my gaze back along the pier to the water at my feet and imagine how satisfying it would be to have conquered that crossing. This is my home ground, this is where I served my apprenticeship, this is where I would like to score my first century.

My research on the English Channel was not wasted effort, clearly much of the advice is transferrable, but there is nothing out there to tell you how to get from Penarth to Clevedon. Other parts of the internet don't cough up much either. Penarth to Weston Super Mare has been done a few times (fewer than 20?), starting with Kathleen Thomas in 1927, fuelled on something like Bovril and chocolate. A small number of stories from more recent years pop up for the Weston route; most successful, but a couple of attempts abandoned because of overwhelming currents. I found a bit on a fundraising site about three chaps from the Welsh side who intended to swim the Penarth to Clevedon route, but no mention of completion of the adventure. Eventually I found a small piece on a local paper's website suggesting that a group of three men had attempted it with only one completing the crossing, but landing way off course in Portishead. A great achievement, but not confidence inspiring for me with my desire to land specifically on Clevedon slipway. All this adds enticement to the challenge, but mostly confirms that I need help.

Of course, I didn't need the internet to find raw, first-hand experience of this swim, and I knew that. There are three people who have swum this route. Steve Price and Jo McCready-Fallon are trustees of Clevedon Marine Lake and Gary Carpenter did it as a local seventeen-year-old lad about a decade ago under the mentorship of Steve. Once I had gathered up the courage to contact Paul the skipper and discuss a realistic and tangible timescale I felt confident enough to announce my intentions to others and begin the beg-for-help process. An encumbrance of unanswered questions was beginning to dampen my desire for the swim, but Steve was as eager to unroll his chart of the channel as I was to start planning. An hour in the pub with Steve and Jo, pointing and pondering over hand-plotted routes of their previous swims, and the starter's pistol was well and truly loaded.

All I need now is a plan.

Enthusiasm and eagerness, of course, do not seamlessly translate to progress. An inherent difficulty with planning and preparing for something of this scale is the sheer abundance of factors which influence the outcome. Some are clear and visible from the outset, but most lurk behind the curtains waiting for their moment to sneak out and sabotage your party, and very few present themselves as a solid building block from the outset, though I put the recruitment of every member of my crew firmly in this category! This ruffian of a channel commands an army of variable elements, many of which will likely only reveal their true nature on the actual day. Yes, a plan of some sort was necessary, but more importantly I felt I needed to develop an 'approach'.

A plan suggests that you are in possession of the full list of required actions, and have sequenced them appropriately, probably even identified the most efficient order and inserted check-points to monitor progress. It feels like a concrete, linear thing, providing reassurance and direction: make all the decisions at the start and off you go. Stick to the plan and it will come good in the end. But this is the stuff of dreams and clearly will not work on a project with this many unpredictable elements. I studied critical path analysis within my degree and applied it many times to bridge projects in my early years as an engineer. It is a fluid and changeable thing, but it does start with a set structure and an ideal order of actions. The beauty of it is that all the actions are nodes in a network of connections – each connection representing the dependency of one action on another. If it is set up well, the model can be adjusted swiftly. An action which fails, or takes longer than expected, is changed and the model flexes and stretches along the dependency lines creating a newly tweaked plan, alerting you to previously unimportant actions which have now crept onto the critical path.

I considered dusting off my old circle templates and steel rule to set about knocking out a PERT chart (this is not a disappointingly diminishing graph which shows how much you physically sag with each passing year, but a Project Evaluation and Review Technique chart – the graphical representation of the nodes and their dependencies). It did not take long to realise the futility of this. I couldn't identify all the nodes – as yet I wasn't sure of the full list of actions ahead of me. I couldn't quite figure out how to incorporate the things which were out of my control. Tides, though predictable, were clearly in charge. The weather came a close second but lacked the predictability. My own physical state is not something I have been confident relying on for a long time. My list of variables was bigger, and considerably more volatile, than my list of factors I could control. And I wasn't at all confident that I had a particularly complete list of either.

Although the end point, the final node, was easily definable, I simply could not pin down enough points in between: I was not clear what was to come my way, who would be there to help me, or how far away I was from being ready. But I had to develop some way of steering my way towards the final goal, so my 'plan' became a combination of simple, basic actions (e.g. swim lots, do research) backed up by developing an approach to dealing with the influencing factors as and when they presented themselves.

I found that I could categorise most of these factors into one of three groups. It would be a turgid process to list and unpick them all here. Some of them will manifest themselves, along with my subsequent action, as you read further: but I shall explore a few now as examples to illustrate the categorisation approach.

Category One was factors which were "beyond my control" but could be dealt with by making a definitive decision. A negative one to mitigate or eliminate the influence, or a positive one to take advantage of it:

- Spring tides flow at up to 7mph – so I decide not to swim on those days.

- Sandbanks breach the surface at certain points in the tidal cycle - so we will plan my start time to cross them when they are at least a metre below the surface or pick a route which takes me around them.

- The slowest flows in the channel (half of those on a spring tide) occur around the neap tides, which is also when the depth of water is changing less rapidly - I will swim then.

Category Two consisted of factors which were again "beyond my control" but were less predictable and could vary in severity. My approach with these was to take strong positive action to reduce their influence should they occur – i.e. increase my chance of success, decrease my chance of failure. This category could come with the subtitle "the harder you work, the luckier you get":

- Weather and sea conditions will please themselves on the day - so I have to train plenty in the toughest I'm willing to take on, find coping strategies and learn my limits. If it's tough on the day, I will know how to adjust. (I could have put this one in the fist category: If conditions are not glassy smooth, I won't swim. I didn't though, and there is more discussion of this later).

- Sea temperature could be lower than the expected average for the time of year – so swim all winter and train for long periods as early in the year as I can, really getting to know how my body copes and how to read my own temperature signals. Build up a bit of extra body mass for thermal capacity and feed well so energy reserves are sufficient for heat generation and propulsion.

- Shoulder injury could hit me. My right collarbone is in two pieces since a ridiculous mountain biking incident, as embarrassing as it was painful. Swimming has been a very important part of the rehabilitation for my shoulder joint, but various bits of the complex mechanism don't quite sit or move as originally designed. Even for an intact pair of shoulders, long distance swims and the volume of training can cause tremendous strain – so get a coach, get my stroke checked out, get some strengthening exercises (and do them!), and get it all from someone who knows their stuff. Don't over-train or stick to a plan for the sake of it. Practise one-armed swimming just in case…….

Category Three was all the things I could control for which I could put in place positive actions to increase my chances of success.

- I expect the swim to take about seven hours if all goes smoothly, but it might not (see above!) - so I needed to train and plan with at least nine hours in mind; if the tide sweeps me beyond Clevedon I could keep going until it turns and brings me back, but only if my crew and I know I've got those extra hours in me.

- Energy use will be huge, and feeding whilst swimming is awkward, but it is within my control – so research types and methods of feed, seek advice, and test it all out in advance in conditions as close to the real thing as possible.

- Decisions to adjust or end the swim will lie with the crew – so communicate well with them, make sure they know what I am capable of physically, what I have prepared myself for, what I am willing to endure. Choose people I have swum with. Give them the best possible chance of making the same decision I would make.

There follow two more major influencing factors worthy of a slightly more detailed analysis. I'll let you decide which category, if any, they fall into:

Tidal flow direction and timings. Incoming tides naturally follow the course of the channel, flowing from the south-west to the north-east, and back again for the outgoing. There is minimal 'slack' water. That will not change for me. Clevedon is directly east of Penarth. That's fixed too. A direct path between the two would therefore cross at about 45 degrees to the direction of flow. Arrival at Clevedon requires high water, or close to it, otherwise I simply won't be able to get to shore. The anticipated duration of the swim is similar to the elapsed time between low and high water. I must choose between using the incoming or outgoing tide to work with. Even on a neap tide I have to accept that a portion of the swim will be spent in water flowing 50% faster than I can swim, no point fighting it, so use it advantageously. Consultation with Steve and Paul leads to using the incoming flow for most of the swim. This means starting about an hour before low water, pointing myself towards Weston (45 degrees south of my destination) and allowing the bulk of the flow to bring me up the channel as I cross it. The outgoing flow option is possible, but the channel is narrower, there are more sandbanks and the Newport and Avonmouth shipping lanes are fully separated and likely to be harder to break free from.

Crew - sourcing and availability. A local swim with a local crew. With such tight restrictions on the timing of the swim, so few windows of opportunity and so much potential for delays and postponements, it was clearly an advantage to have people who were nearby. Stories of whole crews sitting in hotels in Dover for a week waiting for an English Channel window do not sit well with me or my wallet. I'm also very keen not to cause unnecessary inconvenience. I would like a crew who feel invested in my adventure, but do not expect them to raise its importance above their own concerns. Fortunately for me, Steve and Jo were both on-board from the start, which gave me two potential observers for the BLDSA swim recognition criteria. Laura was also keen to crew for the development of her own experience as a coach, and she clearly believes that you get back what you put into the open water world. I had a couple of reserves in mind too. Although the swim was likely to happen during my summer holiday, it would be a working day for most. There is a large swimming community of enthusiastic and generous people based around the lake and sea: I fancied my chances of getting replacements should any of my initial crew fall through.

Decisions

As is probably apparent from above, there are countless of these to be made. Some miniscule, barely decisions at all; answer themselves before you've even finished asking the question. A goodly dose of significant ones; research, canvassing opinion, mulling over time. A fair few on the critical path; deadline to work to, other things on hold until settled.

Two really, really big ones.

Nerves-a-plenty. Round in circles, endless circles. Decided. No, not sure. What if? Confidante required; helpful, but guess what, they're my decisions, not theirs. Pros and cons? Endless lists of pros and cons. Flip a coin. Best of three. Best of five….. come back to it tomorrow.

   ? When (and how) do I tell Jo, my wife, that I am intending to swim across The Bristol Channel?

   ? Do I take Jake, my eldest son, on the boat?

They are, of course, different questions, but both part of the same colossal conundrum.

Family. They are the big spanner you need to maintain the monstrous machine of life.

29

Family. They are, for all the right reasons, the biggest spanner in the works.

Basic risk analysis as a decision-making and planning tool is not complex. Attach a value to the risk, assign another to the consequence, multiply them together and decide if the result is within acceptable parameters. If it is too high, decide no, or return to the risk and see what you can do to reduce it; maybe take another look at the consequence and put something in place to reduce its severity should the risk occur. Bring the product down if you can.

Living with someone who may not want you to do the very thing you are structuring a few months of your life around. Giving them something to worry about, something they have no control over. Trying to operate together as a supportive, loving mum and dad with a restless, agitated elephant wedged in the space between you. Setting up the conditions for the biggest ever, saddest ever, "I told you so" possibly imaginable. How do you put a low number on that?

Watching your dad drown. I challenge you to decide how far up the consequence axis that goes.

This sounds overdramatic, especially here in print, but these were the extents of my fears; uninvited, but not to be dismissed lightly. They acted as a regulator, a baseline to work from, a line not to cross. A point of reference for all the other decisions, a motivator for doing the right thing.

To bring the final product, the decider, down to the lowest magnitude possible, this had to be the safest swim I'd ever done. To take those actions, to tell Jo I intend to do it, and to encourage Jake to be part of my crew, I had to treat every single other decision as a step towards the reduction of those numbers.

I was confident that I wouldn't operate at too high a risk though. To begin with, I was sure that I simply wouldn't do it if it was unacceptably risky. As time and preparation set in, my confidence shifted to an expectation of success, that I would be safe. But Jo, of course, didn't have that insight. So I had to keep her reassured – but how do you describe how effective your planning and contingencies are without acknowledging and discussing the risks themselves?

In the end, biting the bullet was the only way. Sharing my intentions, my goals, my fears and my plans. I know I caused a great deal of worry for Jo. At times I was frustrated by the effort I had to put into reassuring her, could I not simply just be trusted? But that was selfishness on my part. I understand my relationship with the sea, it is somewhere I am comfortable, whereas Jo's is one of avoidance, wariness and anxiety and I had to do my best to respect that. I hope I did.

Jake had to be given the chance to come on the boat. I knew I would regret it bitterly if I didn't ask him. But this does not mean that I had subscribed to the idea that it is always a good idea to have a family member on your support vessel. Yes, you want a crew who care, but they have to understand the adventure, stay rational in the monitoring of the swimmer, know the difference between a downward spiral and a passing dip, make decisions based on rationality, not emotions. Jake has that about him and stood to learn from the experience. I was happy that he would be shielded by the competence and rationality of the rest of the crew and that I would be very, very safe indeed. The fundamental rule of safety was that I would not put myself in danger, and that the crew would not allow it either. So we visit the recurring theme of the decision-making process being in the crew's ownership – relinquishing responsibility to them. As it transpired, I realised that Jake's presence made that easier still for me; the last thing I wanted to do was let him see me stubbornly endanger myself against the advice of the experts on the boat. For all the times I've uttered "Do as you're told!", I owed him the respect of being seen to do the same.

And it all worked out ok. I came home safe. But does that justify my decisions? Would I find them easier to make next time because of it? "We didn't wear cycling helmets in my day, and I survived just fine."; you don't need a degree in critical thinking to spot the flaw in the logic, the broken link between the set-up and the punch-line, but I still regularly hear that delivered with unshiftable, self-righteous conviction. Although my fears were not realised, I still get hit by surges of anxiety over 'What if.......?' moments.

Stroke Development

It would be wrong of me to overlook the basic fact that I swam competitively as a child, though I stopped at fourteen when I was a very different shape from the one lumping about with me now. Returning to swimming some thirty years later the basics were still there, but any understanding of my stroke I may have had as a kid was long since forgotten. As I started to enjoy longer distances in open water and varying conditions it began to dawn on me that many of my 'habits' were counter-productive. Great for a young pair of shoulders impetuously thrashing out bursts of speed over a few lengths, but far from gentle on a neglected upper body wearied by the burden of age, responsibility and public-service. My habitual stroke is now starkly different from a few years ago when I first joined in with a couple of lane sessions. Yes, a high-quality pool swimmer can perform well in the open water and a strong marathon swimmer can probably knock out a surprisingly swift 100m sprint, there is naturally a huge overlap in skills. But they are different disciplines and require resilience in distinct areas.

There are people I swim with who leave me for dead over 200m in the pool, whilst in my jammers I pace their wetsuited self comfortably over a mile in smooth open water. Chuck in some waves and I open up gaps, with time to spare to stop and look around as they catch up. If I join in with a high tempo pool training session, I will ache and twinge for days, whereas the regular session swimmers will be back to do it another three or four times that week. But if I take them for a challenging mile or two in a choppy sea, the consequences are reversed. Don't get me wrong – I am also aware of plenty of swimmers who would outstrip me at both disciplines. I am not claiming to be top of any particular heap, but I have observed enough to know that they are different heaps. Yes, there are differences in the style of fitness training for varying distances, but it is technique which needs the greatest adaptation and customisation for the body you're working with and the conditions you wish to embrace.

What I have focussed on most in developing my swimming is awareness. I try really hard to tune in to signals I receive from my body and from the water I am swimming through. Developing a sense of familiarity for certain positions of limbs, degrees of rotation and areas of pressure from the water. Gaining a sense of when and where the next wave is coming from as the outliers of my body are gently lifted by the beginning of a swell. Knowing exactly how much momentum is needed to allow my arm to continue its path above my head until gravity takes over to return it to the water – realising that my rotation is insufficient if I can feel my shoulder muscles working to lift my arm rather than simply guide it. Watching for bubbles from my hand entry and monitoring the build of pressure as I begin to pull myself forwards. I prefer to coach with focus points, assisted by visualisations. Hundreds of metres of swim-drilling makes you good at swim-drills. Focussing on small technique adjustments a few strokes at a time during your normal swim will allow you to begin re-programming muscle memory in context. As each new tweak becomes more familiar the skills can be layered and worked on together. Patience, practice. This is distance swimming, this is adapting to conditions, we are in it for the long haul. We are ageing, maturing, gaining depth.

A high-quality pool stroke for sprint pace swimming utilises a full range of motion, extends muscles to their extremes and expects them to produce maximum force across the full range of extension and contraction. It is at these extremes where muscles and tendons are at their most vulnerable. Train them well, maintain good technique, and they probably won't let you down over the few hundreds of strokes required of them in the predictable conditions of a 200m pool dash. Try to do the same in an open water marathon swim and expect injury. Those same bits of your body are now expected to repeat those movements tens-of-thousands of times, continuously. There has to be slack built in there somewhere too; over-reach at the front of the stroke with everything stretched to its limit, then a wave rocks your torso, dipping your shoulder and demanding just a couple of extra degrees of movement out of the tired, complex interaction of bone, muscle and sinew. If it's all already at its limit, that may well be the end of your swim. If you get away with it this time, you may not on the next, or the tenth, or the hundredth, or thousandth…….

A formula one car will be borne of the latest tech, the best design team, the biggest investment. Every aspect of its performance optimised to the extremes, no slack, no half-measures: one hundred percent input for one hundred percent output. Top of the heap in every way, the pinnacle of automotive engineering. Bloody useless in the Dakar rally though.

I do not really consider that I have developed "a stroke". I have been working towards a method of swimming which is fluid, changeable, resilient, responsive and adaptive: based on a core set of movements and a default rhythm. It is not finished, never will be, and is not the best out there. But it is the one which so far works for me, the one which allows me to swim even when the sea looks discouraging, the one which will allow me to keep doing this as I age. I have far too many bikes, all different, but my justification is that this allows me more options in how I use them, where I can go. I can travel light and fast(ish) on smooth roads, take on mountain passes with a tent and a spare pair of pants, cruise along filthy tow-paths from café to café, or risk life and limb on the local downhill trails in the woods. All I have to do is wheel the right steed out of the garage. Yes, they all work by pumping up the tyres and turning the pedals, but they are all very different beasts. That's what I have tried to do with my swimming. The analogy clearly isn't perfect, I only have one body (and thus far I haven't upset Jo enough to have to keep it in the garage) and not many options in terms of kit. There is a far starker difference between a one-inch slick racing tyre and a two-inch off road knobbly than there is between a sleek pair of racing goggles and a comfy pair with big, squishy seals. But I have developed a range of options, variations in technique, and I take them all into the water with me on each and every swim. Even as a kid I used to struggle to settle on one thing. I recall "What's the nine-day-wonder-boy up to now?" as a frequent, mildly despairing question from my dad as I threw myself into the next thing to grab my attention, all but abandoning the previous obsession. Sticking with generationally appropriate clichés though, as this unsettledness has tempered with age it seems that I am more "Jack of all trades". This, I am comfortable with (and also with the oft added "master of none"). I can see the attraction of excelling in a specialism, but I also see endless striving and frequent opportunities for disappointment. So I have developed a way of swimming which brings me contentment, which allows me to say 'yes' to anything from a charity sprint relay with some mates through to crossing a beastly channel. I can enjoy myself at a cold-water gala without compromising my readiness for my first big coastal swim in spring. Middle of the road maybe, but it's a nice, scenic road to be in the middle of.

Thus far, this all sounds a bit like I have 'created' something, but that definitely isn't the case. I don't employ any techniques which are not commonly used by others. There is nothing I do which can't be found written about or explained in detailed videos by the full range of outspoken amateurs through to modest experts. There is so much out there; people who have 'invented' strokes; franchised approaches to classifying and working with different styles of swimmer; stroke improvement philosophies to embrace; even the occasional self-proclaimed guru. And a lot of it is good, really good. The bulk of it is ok, but factual rather than useful. Some of it is bad. I have spent many, many hours trawling over books, videos and blogs. I have listened to other swimmers and quizzed them whenever I can. I doubt if I've even managed to absorb one percent of what is out there. What I am certain of is that I have taken nothing at face value. The engineer in me has to be convinced that something is worth trying – I have to be told why it works, and I have to believe that the person offering the explanation understands it. Then I have to test it out to see if it works for me. The time-pressured, modern(ish) adult in me has to be certain that it is sufficiently aligned with what I am trying to achieve to bother persevering with it. So it has pretty much all come down to time. Time spent researching, time spent listening, time spent thinking, but most of all time in the water.

A shortcut to all of this may well have been to seek out some coaching, which is by far and away the best approach to improvement for most people. If you don't have the time, inclination or obsessively introspective approach that I have then a coach is the way to go. A good coach will have broad experience and great knowledge, but most importantly will quickly and effectively identify what you need to work on, in what order and how to get the best out of you. Self-coaching for me was more about the enjoyment of the challenge, a big, fat puzzle. When I first started swimming in open water I had no particular goal in mind or deadline to work to, simply enjoying the developmental process rather than working towards anything was enough. As more time in the water began to bring greater reward and longer swims looked more enticing, that steered me towards resilience more than speed. And then I decided to have a crack at this swim, which brought with it a pressure to achieve a sufficient level of competence. At this point, I could not risk the arrogance of thinking I had sorted myself out perfectly. In fact, I knew that wasn't the case – I had something going on in my basic rhythm which caused niggles around the back of my shoulders after an hour or two. Knowing that my right shoulder is potentially vulnerable thanks to my collar-bone snapping mountain-biking embarrassment, I had to get some expert input. I had swum with Laura; knew how comfortable she is in the very environment I was targeting; seen first-hand at galas the quality of her club swimmers; listened to her story of her tough channel relay in which she ended up doing far more than her fair share and suffered with one shoulder so badly that she pretty much finished it off one-armed. Boxes ticked. I wasn't just looking for a stroke check-up and tune, I knew I needed a coach with me through the mess of preparation, the worry of feed development, the stress of setbacks. I knew my shoulders needed to be strengthened and protected, but had no idea where to start with any form of land-training for this.

One hour in the pool with Laura, a video camera and a bit of poolside space for me to be wrenched, twisted and forced to perform strange movements, and that was that. With expert help I came away with a very specific set of exercises which were easy to work into my normal daily life. They weren't much fun, but they required no more special kit than a length of stretchy rubber, a wall to stand against and a bit of floor to lie on. Fifteen minutes every other day for the next few months and the improvement was gradual, but significant. As my training distances increased, my shoulders felt stronger yet more fluid; better still I could feel the improved connection between my shoulders, back, core, hips and legs. Video of my stroke proved invaluable too as we picked up that, as I tired, on my breathing strokes I would resort to just slightly pressing down with my palm to support my head for a bit longer to breathe. Something I knew to be a common problem but was convinced it was not one of mine. I hadn't picked it up before as that's the one time I can't check what my arm is doing because I'm looking the other way. It felt the same as all the other strokes but was just subtly different enough to put a little extra pressure on the muscles across the back of each shoulder. Easy fix, and something new to concentrate on.

I was very keen after this to secure Laura as my coach for the long haul: someone to come back to if problems developed in my stroke; someone to bounce ideas off for feeds, kit, training methods; someone to swim with me, check out my progress and be my reality check – tell me if I wasn't on track; ultimately be there on the boat to keep me safe and help me adapt to unexpected difficulties. I knew I had Steve to help me too, but there is a surprising amount to do on the boat, especially where the tides demand constant course adaptations. I thought very hard about what I would need to say to Laura to get her to say yes. I needed to convince her that I was worth the effort, likely to see it through. I had a couple of little speeches ready in my head – in the absence of a winning smile or puppy-dog eyes I had to rely on logic and persuasive language. I think I got as far as "I was really hoping you might agree to be my coach for my Bristol Channel swim……..." before she blurted out something along these lines, "Yes, that would be brilliant. When are you hoping to do it? Can I come on the boat? God, I hope I'm not stuck at a gala somewhere! I can come on the boat, can't I? Who else is on the boat? Is it big enough? have you got any pictures of it?"

Team in place. All the support I could hope for, all locally sourced. Time to stop edging towards the idea and ramp it up. Get preparing, get training, get strong, get fit, get focussed. I no longer risk just letting myself down.

Fit for Purpose

Physical fitness for a forty-something is like your shadow. It fades, sometimes disappears altogether. With a dim light casting it onto an irregular surface it can taunt you, its indefinable edges shifting about. Adonis to sofa-slug in a few short paces. Dark and powerful to wispy and weak in the passing of a cloud. Sometimes, when you stand in the clear sunshine on a level, clutter-free surface you can see your best self stretched out on the ground. In those moments, you see what you are capable of and undertake to make the most of it. But life sends in a cloud; perhaps a week of lost training thanks to that inadvertent back-wrench taking the old fridge to the tip. The shape of your shadow gets messy as you lose sleep dealing with ill children and focussed two-mile training swims fade weakly to fuzzy one-milers. A frustrating week at work grinds down your resolve and an extra couple of pints sneak down almost un-noticed, robbing you of the Saturday morning tide. You fcel better as the sun grows brighter and travels higher in the sky, until you glance down to see your shadow mocking you relentlessly, jabbing its accusing, stubby fingers from right down by your feet where it has the most humiliating view of you – oozing waistline capped by burgeoning chins and hairying nostrils.

And what is this 'fitness' we speak of? I do not doubt modern science with its heart rate zones and marginal gains. Triathletes the world over have embraced the power of statistical analysis and the motivational drive of one-upmanship when logging every stroke, pedal and stride. The engineer in me loves what Chris Boardman kick-started in the world of cycling with his scientific approach to taking on the hour record. But I am not looking for a world-beating performance, I am not a world-class athlete, I am competing with no-one but myself and the natural elements. I most definitely do not have endless resources. Time available for training is limited and relatively inflexible, but significantly it is the same time I have at my disposal for seeking out enjoyment – for doing the things which give purpose to getting up and grinding through the working day. Relishing the process is as crucial as the potential satisfaction of completion. Fit for purpose, good enough to do the job; give myself the highest possible chance of success within the limitations of the resources available. Make each chunk of training a joy, not a chore.

For what I have set out to do, fit does not necessarily translate to being the fastest, slimmest, sleekest, most technically advanced super-swimmer I can be. Yes, there are advantages to being faster: the smaller the differential between my speed and the speed of the tide, the more choice and control I have over my route. If, however, that speed comes from over-extending every stroke, working my forty-seven-year-old muscles hard over their maximum range of motion, getting every last degree of joint rotation out of my dodgy right shoulder, then I am setting myself up for a fall. I shall not be trying to speed my way across, pumped on by a 130bpm soundtrack of electronic beats. Nor do I intend to gravel and grind it out to heavy, mournful blues borne of toil and sweat. I shall funk and soul my way across, Craig Charles my DJ: I plan to pedal away on my Hammond Organ when the sun shines on silky-smooth seas, rev up for a sax and horn battle to get me through the choppy chapters, and Otis will be Sittin' on the Dock o' the Bay to bring me home.

My fitness target is simple. Tune my stroke and condition my body so it will work reliably for up to nine hours of swimming in a wide variety of sea conditions, all in a temperature range between 13 and 17 degrees. Hmmm….

Training Regime

An hour in some sort of water, three times a week, or thereabouts. That's as close as I can get to quantifying my normal swimming routine for recent years. I don't train with a club or attend any masters or coached sessions. There is no fixed routine to when or where I swim; in the summer I'll try to make two of the week's swims to Ladye Bay and back (tide allowing and preferably in stirring conditions), maybe one in the pool before work, or perhaps a sunset swim at the lake. Every now and then I might get a free weekend morning aligning with the tide and go beyond Ladye Bay and get a couple of hours in. I have to take what comes. Fortunately, I love swimming in adverse conditions, but this is borne of necessity too; turning my back on chop and swell would at least halve my opportunities to get out there. Winter swim time is about the same, but longer swims in the pool and shorter dips in the cold outdoors.

Three hours a week is the peak rather than the average though; in the logistics of family life, I am not top of the list. Some weeks slip by with nothing, stuffed full of swim club committee meetings, mock exam marking, parents' evenings or galas with the kids. Yes, I will need some consistency to

41

train for this big swim, but I am wary of setting my 'training' goals too high, too early, and hence inconveniencing myself out of contention. With a few months to prepare, I stick with what I know: three swims a week, of at least an hour each. My winter acclimatisation pays dividends as I am swimming comfortably for an hour in the open water by early April. As the real swim approaches, I will increase one of the swims by an hour each week – aiming for a five or six-hour swim a couple of weeks before the real thing. Realistic and achievable. There will be no extra time made available for this though – these are the same windows of opportunity I already use for my current, pleasurable swims; the Venn diagram of "Pleasure Swims" and "Training Swims" must have the largest intersection possible. Whenever I can, I will go about my normal swimming, usual places, familiar company, but maybe a slightly different mindset. I had a little bit of work to do on my technique, but my main concern was simply time in the water, experiencing a full set of conditions. Training swims of specific distances were not a big concern until close to the real event (when most swims are tide affected, distances can be misleading). I had no meterage targets, no specific desire to spend set times in different heart-rate zones or at threshold or grinding through sprint work. I know that working with a variety of pace is important, but I don't need a set or a vibrating watch to boss me about; I can vary my pace during a pleasurable swim, I can respond to conditions or tides, chase another swimmer, pick a different song in my head to swing my arms to for as long as I can recall the lyrics. If I feel strong, I swim strong. If I feel tired, I explore how to maintain my efficiency and work with it. If all is calm, I focus on a bit of my stroke at a time or practise different styles. Trying to mimic other swimmers and testing out their strokes in varying conditions has allowed me to develop my own bank of styles enormously. This can all be done during my usual swims.

As it turned out, three swims a week worked out well. Manageable and enjoyable. There was a little extra pressure to make sure I got the swims in; a few early mornings I may not have bothered with otherwise. Time on my bike gave way to time in the water on an increasingly frequent basis and I stopped cycling altogether in the last few weeks (the backs of my shoulders struggled to recover from the longer swims if I cycled on my non-swim days). In the week I had a three-hour swim scheduled I just so happened to be taking a group from Lulworth cove to Durdle Door and back, so to get my time in I put in an extra 30 minutes along the beach while the rest of them let their lunch settle. Splashing about in Stair Hole; swimming backstroke under the arch at Durdle Door; dragging myself through the thick, shiny fronds of weed to get to Bathole Caves; stopping to take group selfies from the water with the spectacular cliffs in the background. This did not feel like training. My aim was for training to be "swimming with training in mind" rather than "swimming to a training plan". This is not a new approach for me, I went with it because I've done it before for cycling challenges, and I know it worked.

Skinny and wiry-tough, my teenage self could deliver more than my physical appearance suggested, but I was keen to look the part too. These were the (dark) days of sleeveless vests and cut-off jeans for shorts, so there was nowhere to hide my pipe-cleaner limbs. A couple of years chucking free-weights about in the hope of bulking up a bit taught me a few things, made me stronger still, but did not change the fact that people noticed my elbow long before my hint of bicep came into view. As the denim of my shorts frayed, my legs merged into the mess of cotton danglers like noodles in a bowl of spaghetti. Somewhere in that period though, I acquired a book about body-building by Bill Richardson (no relation!). I read it very carefully and amongst all the advice for 300lb bodybuilders I hunted out the bits I felt I could apply to my 150lb self. Focus. Concentration.

Intent. Clarity of outcome. If it's a bicep curl you are doing, then isolate the movement with your technique, don't dissipate the energy to slight movements or wobbles of unrelated muscles. Work the stabilising muscles too (free-weights rather than machines) but try to keep the dynamic movement in the focus muscle. Watch what you are doing, use a mirror if necessary, engage your brain in the process, tune in carefully to the feedback your senses are giving you. If your brain knows why you are lifting that particular weight in that specific way, then it will focus your body's resources appropriately and construct a memory of it. It will come to recognise the signals it receives when it does it successfully, respond automatically when it senses a problem, know how to regulate the energy supply and timing of power input; increase chance of success, reduce potential for injury.

It's the closest I can get to mindfulness. Swimming does feel like a kind of meditation for me; I can always find something to focus on, something more important at that moment in time than whatever fusses and frustrations I got into the water with. A long swim – rotation and relaxed arm recovery to keep stress off my shoulders. A choppy swim – experiment with stroke rate and sighting frequency to match the rhythm of the sea. Glassy smooth surface – clench my buttocks, tighten my core and tune my two-beat kick with the smallest of flicks. Speedy companions – get every catch and pull right, focussing on the build of pressure.

I do pay very careful attention to my stroke when I swim. Yes, I was a club swimmer as a kid, but not beyond the age of fourteen and I never troubled the headlines, but clearly the basics were lodged somewhere in my mental murk. As a teenager I would run the mile to the sea, swim the length of Appley Beach (Ryde, Isle of Wight) and back, then run home again, but only in the summer and not that often. From the time I left home for university until my eldest son was nine and joined Backwell Swimming Club, I don't think I did anything at all which I would now count as a swim. That's nearly two decades to forget how to do it. A few swims in a spare lane while the boys were training, some carrots dangled by a few friends to tempt me into the open water and the bug sank its teeth in good and proper. But what to do with it? I have no desire to strut up to the blocks, slap my chest and thighs and try to shave hundredths of a second off my 100m time. I don't run, so triathlon is out. Mass events stress me out – they feel like being at work. But I like to swim purposefully, I like to be aiming for something with a sense of tangibility. I do not need a competitor number, start-time or a pre-determined route map. I do need something which demands a wide-ranging strategy, something which could go this way or that, such that the training has to be varied: focussed as much on broad resilience as raw output. My motivation for this challenge stays high because I am enjoying the preparation, I am trying to cover all bases; these are skills which could take me way beyond just this crossing. If it all falls through, I'll be ready for something else.

With only five weeks to go I am happy with my training so far. I have comfortably done my three-hour swim, there's been plenty of rough stuff to hurl myself about in. My bank of stroke adaptations has grown in variety and scope and I have sought opportunities to fight, work with, cut across, and submit to a full-on feast of different chop, waves, swell, tide, flow, wind and temperature. My stretches and strengthening exercises have been ongoing and thus far I am injury free and feel strong. The nutritional side of my training has also yielded a successful gain of about a stone, liberally distributed to hopefully provide a little extra insulation and energy reserves for the long haul. So I am confident I can make it half-way across, but I have yet to train and test my plans for the toughest bit – the last few miles. Time to broadcast the pilot episode of my feeding regime, properly monitor and quantify my swim speed, and scrutinise what my body does as it tires. A focus group of one – feedback essential to secure the series.

The first window of tidal opportunity for the actual crossing is a three-day period of 2nd, 3rd and 4th August, a couple of weeks in to my summer holiday. This gives me a few days to recover from the inevitable physical wipeout which comes at the end of every term, but with brutal abundance at the very end of the school year. A tapering, chilled-out week before the attempt with a couple of gentle swims and plenty of good food and I should be ready. My last three big swims are by necessity distance based rather than time based. Working backwards from 2nd August, this puts the 10-mile swim on Monday 24th July, 8 miles on Sunday 16th July and 6 miles on Sunday 9th July.

Much as I would like these to be in the sea, in the conditions I can expect for the real thing, there are compelling reasons to do these in the lake. Anything more than 3 hours in the sea here is very difficult because of the tides; without an accompanying boat the only choice is to travel along the coast and back with the incoming and outgoing tide. Getting in and out more than a couple of hours before or after high water is very difficult without trying to cross mudflats and grapple with a very fast stream. I also need to test my feeds but can't carry them with me. Most importantly I need to monitor and record my swim speed and how it changes over time and distance. My course across the channel cannot be planned or adjusted on the day without the decision makers on the boat having a good grasp on the speed I am likely to maintain at each stage of the journey and tide. Even with an accurate tracker of some sort, any speed data from being in the tidal sea will be useless. The lake it is.

Clevedon Marine Lake is about 250m long if swimming close to and parallel with the seaward wall. At the end of the lake at which I prefer to change and leave my stuff there are some railings extending a few metres out along the lake wall. Exactly 161 metres from the end of these railings an aluminium bracket has been stuck to the wall. Ten of those is a mile. On Sunday 9th July, sometime before 7:00 am, lake to myself after inadvertently frightening away the heron on the pontoon: I lay out my prepared first run of test feeds, slip into my jammers and gently pootle out into the lake to secure my tow float to the bracket with a cable tie, giving me a tangible and easily visible target at each end of the tenth of a mile. That's my Sunday morning entertainment sorted! Sixty of those in batches of ten, guzzling down some strange liquid and noting down the time between each batch.

A mile or two in, and a couple of regulars have popped down for their Sunday morning dip. I probably appear a little unsociable as, although exiting the water to feed, I am trying to mimic the real situation in other respects by knocking it back quickly and get the time for the previous mile scribbled down in about thirty seconds. Back in the water, restart the stopwatch on my trusty Timex, and off I go again for a very slow count to ten. I have included the reports on my 6-mile and 8-mile swims in an appendix, they note times, practicalities and comments on my physical state, but what they don't include is how lovely it was to be joined in the water by a familiar face, Claudia. Of course, I couldn't stop to chat, and our differing speeds meant there was little more than an occasional passing exchange of grins, but what a difference that made to my mental state. I can honestly say that those long-distance repetitions of the same 161m stretch of water are the dullest, most mentally testing swims I have ever done. My only other entertainment was an on-off relationship with some sort of sea creature each time I turned by my tow float. I have no idea what it was, but I guess it was as curious about me as I was about it. No chance of setting eyes on it in the silty water, but most times I stopped and turned it came and bumped my leg. The "will it, won't it?" question gave me something to think about on my way along the wall. I suffered crushing feelings of rejection and disappointment on the "it won't" occasions; emotional fragility is definitely a hazard of long-distance swimming.

As recorded in the notes of my 6-mile swim, I did not feel great for the rest of the day, but it informed the adaptations for the following week, and so I returned seven days later for eighty repetitions of the railing/bracket journey. And this time, I have my very own pair of too-brief swim-briefs to test out. They have arrived, and as with everything else I cannot leave it to the day of the swim to discover their inadequacies, so the jammers are rested. In at 7:00am, no heron this time but otherwise very similar to the previous week; Claudia made an appearance, but no bumps from below. This swim felt significantly better than the previous week: no repeat of the stomach issues and the last two miles, though slower, felt no harder than the previous few. Most encouragingly, I strolled out of the lake after the eighth mile unspent, plenty more in the tank and feeling stronger and more robust than a week earlier. The trunks test was definitely worthwhile. It has not been committed to paper, but I emerged from the water with a very clear map of where I would need to apply lubricant to my skin, having needed to do so at the four-mile mark. Significantly, the inner parts of the tops of my thighs, unshielded by the usual leg-length of my jammers, had clearly had a bit of a tiff and rubbed each other up the wrong way. Other roughed-up patches were focussed wherever the edges of the trunks contacted my skin. The severity of chafing in each area being directly proportional to the level of awkwardness if asking someone else to apply the protection. Not all the damaged patches of skin bordered the allotment though, if I hadn't applied petroleum jelly, I would definitely have lost skin towards the back of my armpits. This is new to me this year, and not just because of the increase in the length of my swims. My shoulders are not especially broad for my height, but the volume of swimming and the changes to my stroke style have resulted in my lats and triceps gaining some bulk. Without a great deal of width for them to occupy, they compete heavily for space at the very back of my stroke. As my hand heads for the exit point, I can feel my triceps shortening and widening and pushing my lats out of the way. I can adapt my stroke to avoid it, and it is rarely an issue early in a swim when my rotation is at its best, but as I tire it happens more often. It is also the case that my basic habitual stroke, the one which happens without thought or concentration, has been ingrained over the past couple of years as a slimmer man. Without a doubt, the additional pounds I have acquired in the last three months have had to spread themselves about my body and occupied places which were previously spaces: my armpits as fair game as anywhere else. One last little patch to deal with, again exacerbated by my new insulating layer, is in the creases of my neck, just below my jaw but only on the left side. This bugs me a little as it suggests an asymmetry in my stroke which I have been unable to pinpoint, but it's also possibly the difference in angle between my neck and shoulders thanks to my broken right collarbone. No matter, I will definitely be pulling on a pair of surgical gloves and slapping on oodles of lube on the boat before the swim. Not glamorous, but neither is climbing out early and raw. This is what the long preparation swims are for, anticipating and mitigating the potential problems.

Just the 10-mile training swim to go.

Feed Development

There is a vast amount of information, experience and expert knowledge available to get you started on sorting out your endurance swim feeding regime. A few of the more scientific articles held my attention for a while, but it didn't take long to realise that I just needed to know what was worth trying out and get on with testing it. There is a lot to think about here: not just what you consume, but how much and how often, how it's delivered, how it is managed on the support boat, and what to do if it needs adjusting.

Most important of all is to test everything, thoroughly, in conditions as close to the real thing as possible. It is very easy to find stories of failed or difficult swims because the feeding went wrong. This is not a normal eating environment, yet energy and fluid supplies are crucial. Your body is horizontal and immersed in cold water. You are trying to stay warm and exert energy to swim effectively over a long period. You cannot sit down, chew carefully on your food and then give it time to settle. Gravity is usually on your side working stuff through your system, but horizontal in the water, probably being lurched about, there are extra challenges. The middle of your swim is not the time to discover that orange squash makes you retch, or maltodextrin turns your lower intestine into a water flume. It's not just you in the water either – how are the crew going to prepare your feed? A wet, windy, rocky boat is not an easy place to measure out powder and mix precise volumes of liquid.

From the multitude of available advice, the apparently generally accepted knowledge, and a couple of chats with Laura and Steve, I started with these basics:

- Understand and respect the practicalities of feeding in the Bristol Channel.

- Feed regularly, right from the start (fuelling for the future), to give time for the body to distribute the energy effectively and replenish energy as it is used.

- Have reserves of energy available (fat) and train such that your body learns how to access it.

- Find a powder-based mix of glucose sources (maltodextrin being the starting point) to take on board regularly.

- Incorporate stuff I know works for me (from previous endurance bike rides I know that I cope best with eating regularly and including lots of protein such as eggs and nuts.)

- Make sure to include treats of some sort. A cup of tea and a bacon sandwich would be ideal!

- Have a good meal before the swim.

Start with what I know. A good dinner will see me through three hours of swimming. A really good dinner will get me through three hours without too much deterioration in my energy output or slowing of my swim speed.

Beyond three hours and my performance will be made or mashed by the success of my feed regime. My understanding of how effective it will be beyond three hours can't develop until I do a swim that long, having fed to a plan specific enough to evaluate. If it were a bike ride, I would stop, take my time over solid foods I know I enjoy, mostly savoury and plenty of protein. One hundred and three miles of mountain biking with twelve thousand feet of climbing on rough chalk bridleways across the South Downs was fuelled by pasties and home-made flapjack crammed with dried fruit, nuts and sugar; washed down with lots and lots of water. This clearly won't work in this environment.

This isn't so easy. Out in the water I can't stop for long, no picnic table adorned in gingham, no silver cutlery or side plate. I'll be bobbing or lurching about in whatever conditions the channel has settled on at that moment, unable to make contact with any solid surface bar the containers for my feed. Most food solids are pretty much impossible to get down whilst treading water and my body won't hold on to or process food in its usual way while I am rolling about on my stomach in the water. Unable to down a pint and a reliably slow eater, this is going to be a significant part of the challenge. I decide on feeding every thirty minutes to reduce the volume I need to take on at any one time, but it has to happen in less than a minute to avoid excessive drift in the strong tidal stream and give myself the chance of completing the swim in one tide cycle. "Maxim" is the magic potion most channel swimmers apportion a large chunk of their success to: it is based around maltodextrin. This is easily available as a powder and is useful for this purpose as it digests and is absorbed quickly by the body. That's my starting point. How much is required is also difficult to assess as we all output energy at different rates when we swim, and it can vary hugely with sea temperature and conditions. Assessing other peoples' experiences leads me to start my testing with an intake of 100g per hour (99g of carbohydrate yielding 396/kcal according to the packaging). Fluid intake is also hard to pin down, but I start with about a litre every two hours as the basis of my system. The maxim powder will be dissolved in water, but I decide to do this fairly concentrated with water alongside so that I can vary liquid intake without affecting the energy intake.

My first chance to begin testing this all properly is the 6-mile swim I have planned in for 9th July. I've done a bit of mixing of maltodextrin with different flavourings and swigging some to check it goes down and stays down ok, but it's not until I'm swimming for longer than three hours that it can be fully assessed for repeated intake and effective energy supply. In agreement with advice from Steve, a small dash of blackcurrant makes the mixture palatable without the build-up of acidity from something orange or lemon based. My initial test feed is:

- 100g Maltodextrin in 200ml water, dash of blackcurrant, at 1 hour in, then every half hour.

- 100ml water available at every feed – have as much as I feel I need.

- A banana at some point – I like them!

- Some soft, dried apricots once during test swim – recommended by many swimmers (as are tinned peaches which by all accounts slip down easily).

- Warm, sugary tea part way through and at the end – a treat for me, but I also find it combats the effects of salt on the inside of my mouth and throat.

- Finish with a nut-based cereal bar (wouldn't use during actual swim, but I find a small protein input helpful after prolonged exercise).

All this is detailed in the report of this test swim in the appendix, but there were some very useful outcomes which allowed me to make adjustments in time for the 8-mile test swim a week later. I had a normal lunch after the swim but spent the afternoon with some stomach cramps and a very unsettled digestive system. This seemed as much to do with the volume of liquid intake without any real solid to counter it, though possibly also the aggressively fast digestion of the maltodextrin. The banana was good, though I didn't think I could eat it quickly enough in solid form out in the middle of the channel. The tea was a huge winner: it went down well but was also a real treat I found myself looking forward to. Protein was definitely necessary, but I was keen to avoid a supplement in the feed liquid, so a solid source was needed. Though I'm normally quite keen on the apricots, I dumped those straight away – too slow to eat and did not sit well in my stomach. I drank all the water, so need more available, but did feel bloated after three feeds so still need the option of cutting it down on occasion without losing out on energy supplements.

By now I knew that my swim would start early in the morning, so breakfast would be the pre-swim meal. Porridge has always been my choice for the start of a day of exercise. Oats are known for their slow-release energy, something which I felt I could do with alongside the fast-absorbed powders to avoid rocketing spikes of energy through the swim. They are also absorbent and soften in liquid, so I was keen to incorporate them in my energy intake somehow. At the same time as ordering a huge packet of dextrose powder, I added a couple of bags of finely ground porridge oats (Scottish) to the basket. A bit of experimentation led to an easily drunk mix of 50g oats and a spoonful of honey in 250ml of water mixed thoroughly in the blender; an experimental spoonful of peanut butter in one of the test batches hit the back of my throat stickily and got an early rejection buzzer. Laura suggested I tried a mix of dextrose and maltodextrin, as dextrose is absorbed slightly faster and is often thought to be a touch easier on the stomach, and also to reduce the energy content a little as I swim efficiently and seem able to stay warm for long periods in the water without depleting my energy supplies too much. I decided to go with eggs for the protein, hard-boiled being the only practical method I could think of. The 8-mile swim is clearly going to be an hour longer, so a more thorough test, but on a refined model:

- 40g Maltodextrin, 40g Dextrose in 250ml water, dash of blackcurrant, at 1 hour in, then every half hour.

- Half a banana near the beginning.

- Half a boiled egg on two occasions.

- Porridge oat and honey smoothie (water-based) at about three hours in.

- Warm tea every now and then.

Overall, this was a much more successful trial than the previous week. Significantly, I felt less tired and in far better physical condition for the rest of the day. The energy mix went down easily. The oat smoothie was instantly settling and just felt right both to drink and to swim with. I still wanted banana in there but still didn't fancy trying to eat it normally whilst treading water, so I incorporated it into the oat and honey smoothie. The egg was a success but required a very specific technique. Chewing was too slow and slippery egg has a habit of rolling about in the mouth in chunks just too small to trap between teeth, but just too large to swallow. So, a couple of quick bites to start the breakdown, then liquidise it by forcing it a couple of times through slightly open teeth, slug it down, swig of water, job done. Middle of the sea? Yes. Dinner table? NO!

Although I didn't get to test a further time as my 10-mile training swim never came to fruition, this was good enough for me to concoct a final feed plan for the actual day, which is in an appendix along with the annotated record of what I actually consumed on the day.

All this testing was done stood on solid ground between each mile of my training swims, so the next job was to work out how to make it work from the moving boat, with me in the water. I decided to pre-prepare as much as possible, so the crew did not have to measure or mix on the boat. Again, I had studied other people's methods of getting the various items from the boat to the swimmer. I chose a basket method which could deliver

500ml water bottles or solid items in a removeable plastic cup, all to be dangled from an extending decorators' pole designed for paint-rollers. The prototype used a paint caddy in which I created compartments by sticking in the bottom halves of 1 litre drinks bottles. An hour in the lake with a useful bit of windy chop across the surface gave me the opportunity to put it through its paces. Laura came along to monitor my stroke rate and dangle the basket of feed on each lap for us both to practise. Seems ok, but it looks like I'll be nearer to a minute guzzling stuff; rushing for thirty seconds just seems to fill me with air and the next few minutes of swimming are belchy, retchy and uncomfortable. I don't actually bring the feed back up, but it gets close. When I take a few extra seconds to take it on board and let it settle, I am comfortably back into my rhythm almost straight away. Fine tuning, but significant: no value in a carefully tested and concocted feed being ejected into the channel to leave me under-nourished later in the swim. The paint caddy almost worked, but I struggled to lift a couple of the feed bottles out of the compartments as the handle of the bucket got in the way. Rectangular seemed like a more promising way to go.

Ten minutes in the pound shop, an hour or so in the garage melting holes in plastic pots and baskets with the soldering iron, a few minutes with some cable ties and I have an improved contraption. A rectangular basket allowing easier access to lift the bottles out. Compartments for the feed/smoothie/tea bottles made from slightly more sturdy and smooth-sided plastic soup tubs. Some smaller tubs which drop into the top of those for holding boiled eggs or ibuprofen and a ring of pipe lagging wrapped around so it can be floated if the sea is calm enough. Not significantly different from the tested prototype, but all marginal gains of one sort or another.

Preparing the feed for the real event was easy in the kitchen. I had decided to prepare and plan for up to eight hours of swimming, and it would be over to the crew to take it from there if we were still going after that. The whole system is based around 500ml water bottles, but with only 300ml or less of liquid in them meaning that they could be given a good shake before being placed in the basket and handed out to me. With a couple of spares of each thrown in, this meant preparing 13 bottles of "maldex" energy feed, 13 bottles of just water, 5 bottles of oat smoothie, and having 4 bottles ready for the warm tea to be put in. Spare packets of powder and spare water went on the boat too. The warm tea was about the only thing I decided the team would have to make on the boat, and although there was a kettle on Ruby D we decided to use a 5 litre flask with a pump-action top for the hot water – this also allowed the crew to put a shot of hot water in my feeds to make them a little more palatable from my dining position of the cold sea. Chuck in some pre-halved boiled eggs, a bag of jelly babies, a tube of electrolyte tablets and some ibuprofen and that's me catered for. Of course, I chucked a load of cereal bars, snacks and a couple of sandwiches in, so I would have something to eat on the boat if I had to abandon the swim.

Conclusions and advice for anyone else? Listen to others, but only use that to give you a start point. Listen to your body and try to work in the things you like, the food which makes you feel good, the stuff you look forward to. Finally – test everything. And test it again.

On the subject of swimwear

Skip this bit if you have recently eaten.

I swim in jammers. If I could swim in something which disguised the shape of my body more effectively, without restricting me or slowing me down, I would. Once in the water, submerged and out of sight, I am a much happier man. I have a wetsuit, and have grunted my way into it often enough to conclude that I am too lazy to wrestle with it before, during, and after swims. Neither am I keen on parading around looking like an unevenly extruded black pudding. This is a personal thing, I have absolutely no issue with everyone else swimming in whatever they choose, it is simply about what gets you in the water. Sometimes, when faced with the single-figure temperatures of winter, I contemplate wriggling back into neoprene, but I can't balance the extra 20 minutes of faffing about for the sake of a swim which may be a few minutes longer, yet is still too short for me to count as exercise. My winter swims are for the afterglow, and for sustainment of habituation and acclimatisation; they extend my outdoor distance training season by about six weeks at either end. A near-naked dip will do.

Originally, my own self-satisfaction was to be sufficient validation of the swim and I would have been happy splashing my way across in my usual get-up: a cap, some goggles and my jammers. I was confident I could manage the time in the water without a wetsuit and over that distance would much prefer the freedom of movement skins swimming affords. All I had to do was choose my outfit. A Clevedon Lake and Sea Swimmers cap adorned with Nancy Farmer's striking pier design; the orange one probably as it seems less inclined to wriggle its way up my head than the blue one. Some silicone putty earplugs. A pair of Speedo Futura Biofuse goggles; clear, tinted or polarised; which pair would be a decision on the day, but no doubt the others would be on the sub's bench hoping for a change in conditions and a swift call-up. And to keep the sun off my bum? Well I like jammers! They extend part way down the thigh and place the seams and hems well away from any nooks, crannies or areas of potential rubbing – this I consider perfect for long swims in salty water where unfortunate chafing might end a swim before fatigue. At the price point of my swimwear I am not afforded any advantage in performance over a pair of briefs through any hydrophobic properties, muscular compression or thermal insulation. I have two pairs of TYR jammers which have been through four years of regular pool swims, many, many miles in the sea and lake, frequent cycles in the washing machine (in direct contradiction of the care instructions), and still conceal the texture, if not the form, of my central embarrassments. Significantly, they have held their shape during this time far better than I have. It was to be a tough choice as to which of this faithful duo I would choose on the day; I even considered a half-way swap so as not to offend either pair. A subtle shift in focus however, condemned them both to be left in the bottom of my KitBrix.

Steve is heavily involved with the British Long Distance Swimming Association (BLDSA) and suggested that getting some recognition, validation, and a certificate for the swim would be worthwhile (he was right). It is a route recognised by the BLDSA thanks to Steve, and as such has now had three people complete it under their guidelines. All that was required to bring my outfit plan in line with their criteria was a re-imagining of the trunkage. The BLDSA state quite clearly that "......the costume must not extend lower than the crotch onto the upper leg". Jammers simply will not do. Having never forked out more than £20 for jammers, which contain enough material to cover 'thighs' and 'things', I figured that would be a perfectly reasonable budget for a briefer version containing barely enough material to cover just the 'things'.

Equipped with my budget and a cup of tea, it was time to shop. All I wanted was plain black briefs with sides about 6 inches deep to cover my hips. There were plenty of pairs the right shape, but all subject to the current trend of boastfully attracting attention to themselves and their contents with (s)wanky colours and patterns, plus a premium of an extra tenner for the privilege. Almost all the plain briefs I could find were very narrow at the hips. The first problem with such brief briefs is that the narrow hip line pulls the crotch-ward edge of the leg holes upwards, increasing chafing in sensitive areas. The second problem with such scanty skimpies is that in a passer-by's peripheral vison they can often fear full nakedness has just been observed, resulting in a more focussed, instantly regrettable look allowing the full horror of the scene to hit their retinas. Hurried shielding of nearby children's eyes is an inevitable consequence. I am a schoolteacher. I cannot go around being the cause of this.

After many, many, seemingly eternal minutes of trudging from shop to shop (on-line, of course) the best I could find were some 5-inch briefs, mostly black and with a couple of slabs of primary colour on the hips, just in budget. I do not like wearing them. My relationship with swimwear has gone beyond early romance; I much prefer it these days with the lights off. All the pairs of briefs I have tried, including these, unpleasantly accentuate the very things middle-aged men like myself would rather just kid ourselves aren't visible. The absence of a younger man's buns means that we have developed a gravity-driven fold where our buttocks finish and our legs begin. Briefs do one of two things; they either disappear upwards into this fold, uncomfortably, and accentuate the way our flaccid cheeks hang, clearly hankering to pop down and say hello to our heels; or they take the high road and pass above it, creating a double-cheeked monstrosity. A hefty double-butt may be a welcome sight on a welded girder, but not in my back yard. As for the vegetable patch in my front garden, well I would prefer to subtly screen my prize courgette from frost and passing glances with a large, thick tarpaulin rather than shrink-wrap it for display.

I did already own a pair of plain black, brief trunks. Very brief. Only about 2 inches at the sides. They hover uncomfortably close to the boundary between swim-briefs and thongs. And, yes, I do sometimes wear them for swimming. Before the shout of "hypocrite" bursts forth I must assure you that this is done in a measured and respectful way. For the coldest of cold swims, perhaps sub 5 degrees, these are one of my two small concessions to extra winter kit. Along with the well-known practice of "double-hatting" to insulate my head a little better, I also occasionally use my "bib and tucker" technique. We are all aware that heat loss is greatest through our extremities thanks to a greater ratio of surface area relative to the encapsulated volume. Consequently, the sharpest, swim-ending pain is also felt in these physical outliers. The briefs go on before my jammers with the specific purpose of keeping any such vulnerable extremities closer to a source of warmth and reducing the exposed surface area. In such circumstances, using this method, I can exit the water proclaiming, truthfully, "I can't stay in any longer, my fingers hurt too much!"

Clearly, I should have more significant things to think about in the preparatory months than my swim-apparel, but had I considered it just a little longer I may have been able to anticipate (though probably not mitigate) the public consequence of revealing my choice. Engaging my friends in the swim groundwork using social media turned out to be a double-edged, blunt and rusty sword. A genuine level of interest convinced me to set up the page so that my friends could support me with, and keep tabs on, my progress through the training and preparation. I was anticipating encouragement, advice and inspirational conversation flowing from a vast treasury of experience and curiosity. However, the first mention of the brevity of my swimwear on the social media group was akin to pulling the plug on the dam. Floodgates wide open. Formerly quiet observers of the gentle flow of informative posts became tabloid journalists with sleaze story quotas to reach. I'd log on expecting questions about my training schedule or current thinking on feeds and tides, but I got stuff like this……

"Oh strewth! I've just read he's doing it in budgie smugglers!"

Jeremy Murgatroyd

"Who smuggled the first budgie. Why budgie? And why down THERE? Beaks. Claws. OW!!!".

Michelle Walker

I should have known.

It is possible that you now suspect I have 'issues' with brief swimwear beyond that which is normally considered rational. Many people are perfectly comfortable in them, so perhaps I should just get over it. That is probably true, but this is deep-seated and can be explained by lemon meringue pie and old episodes of The Sweeney. There is a shade of yellow which can normally only be found on the glossy surface of the lemony layer of a cheaply manufactured lemon meringue pie. Bank robbers and the like, in The Sweeney, were generally facially unblessed and uncomfortable to look at. That discomfort level would increase several-fold as they readied themselves for action by squeezing their hefty features into an eyebrow-twisting, nose-squishing stocking. It is a combination of these two things, somewhere deep in my swimming history, which has left me in this possibly irrational state.

Precisely where and when is no longer in my memory and largely irrelevant, but I was young, I was at a swimming pool, and I wanted to get out. As I headed for the lethal, toe-slicing metal steps in the corner of the pool, getting close enough to reach out for the handrail, a figure deftly slid across from my left and planted their foot on the bottom rung, thus forcing me to wait my turn. I was young enough to consider almost everyone else as old, but this man was way up there at the top of the tree. He was small and thin, far too small and thin to properly accommodate the mass of bodily wrinkles he had been allocated. Clearly having blown all his energy on the dash for the steps, I stood and waited as he weakly raised himself up out of the water, stopping to catch his breath on each rung. As he hoisted himself once more, enough to reveal his trunks to the world, I was dealt with the visual equivalent of chewing a live slug. Whatever it was that he had chosen to use as swimwear, I do not believe to this day that it was available in the shops. Lemon meringue pie yellow in colour, minimal in coverage, stocking-thin in substance and, of course, wetly transparent. I recall the feeling of panic, I doubt I quite understood what I was experiencing but I know I was increasingly desperate to get out of the pool to somewhere else, somewhere away from this unsettling moment. Eager to get my eyeline to a safer height, and believing that the old man was now about to clear the top of the steps, I grabbed the handrail and launched myself upwards to make a dash past him.......

.......but it seems he was not quite ready to move on. Supporting himself on the handrails, swapping his hands over as he did so, he turned back to face the water just exited as if to wave to someone still in the pool. And there it was, my dash for safety had not only failed but plunged me further into the depths of horror. Just as I successfully propelled myself upwards, my face met his, but not the face on the front of his head. I was eye-level to the front of his trunks, nose to nose, only inches away. I promise you there was a Sweeney bank-robber's face in there, nose squished against the straining material, deep, dark shadows for the eye sockets and the wildest of twisted monobrows. I thank the stars and Poseidon himself that it was not actually a stick-up, but nonetheless I was robbed of something that day.

Chapter 4

WAITING TO SWIM

F ive days of teaching left in the school year and I can feel the inevitable deterioration begin to take hold. No matter how hard I try, year in, year out, I limp over the finish line and collapse onto the stretcher of the first weekend of the summer holidays. I know exactly how it will be, I will be in no fit state for anything: simple conversations feel like an interrogation in a deep, dark bunker; anything but the gentlest of televisual comedy seems like an assault on my senses, battering me with crassness and irritation. Every one of my antibodies packs its bags and stuffs off, leaving me vulnerable to any and every contagious illness within my postcode. Decisions, oh, decisions – what new torture is this? Would I like a cup of tea? How do I know? What are the criteria? What if I say yes and it turns out I didn't want one? I'm still only fifteen minutes into trying to decide if I need a pee – I can't cope with the tea dilemma until I've got to grips with this widdle-wondering...... This is why I scheduled my 10-mile swim for the Monday rather than the Sunday: time enough for a re-boot, a deep discharge and full recharge, re-configure the operating system and apply all the updates. As I approach the end of the teaching week, I am aware that something has got me. It's not a cold, I don't quite have a cough, sore throat or runny nose. I ache though, lights are brighter than usual, sounds are sharper and more intrusive, the stairs are steeper, and my limbs are heavy. My head isn't quite throbbing with pain, but I can feel my pulse beneath my scalp.

On the last day of term a few of us usually take advantage of the slightly early finish and do an informal triathlon – a swim in the lake, a ride round the local country lanes, a jog along the coast (I volunteer to stay behind and guard the bikes for this bit), and dinner in the pub. This year we are beset with wind and rain, which would normally disappoint me, but not stop me from getting on with it regardless. This time around I am wary, I have something larger at stake and decide to play it safe. So much has been invested in my upcoming swim that I daren't risk it for a bit of bravado – throwing myself into arduous conditions when I can feel I am vulnerable to some sort of illness. Under the weather I can cope with. Under the doctor risks decisions about my swim being taken out of my control. It is just shy of two weeks until the first tidal opportunity and I still have a ten-mile training swim to do.

I am generally of the opinion that if we only train when we're at our best, we can't train enough to improve, and neither are we preparing ourselves for the inevitability of having to perform at reduced capacity. I very much doubt I will be at 100% on the day of the swim itself: if nothing else I am unlikely to have had a good night's sleep. There is a lot at stake here though, and this is a specific decision, not a general principle. Sunday evening comes around, I am not right, no worse but no better, and I am scheduled to be in the lake at 7:00am for the first of the one hundred railing to bracket repetitions. This is a bigger decision than a cup of tea and I'm only just beginning to settle back onto a path parallel to rationality. I imagine getting up at 6:00am the next morning – done with eagerness on the previous Sundays, but filling me with dread this time around. My body shouts louder than my brain: twinges, shivers and listlessness telling me to stay in, wrap up and let my systems sort themselves out. I exchange a few messages with a couple of friends who are similarly drawn to physical exploits and decide that the 10-mile swim can wait a couple of days. If I'm still not up to it by Wednesday, then I'll bin it altogether as that wouldn't leave me time to recover and taper before the 2nd August. This feels risky, but I console myself with how strong I felt only a week ago after the eight miles, there were definitely more miles left in the tank. Right now, it is my health which is off track, not my swimming readiness, so that is where my resources must be directed.

So begins ten days of jitteriness. Apprehension, nerves, excitement, self-doubt, guilt, impatience, dread, frustration, indecision, more self-doubt. I leap between them all, like stepping stones in a pond full of snapping alligators. I can't settle on anything, constantly confusing myself with mid-range weather forecasts, frustrated that the day I wake up feeling fully well just doesn't seem to come. Normally, I'd head out for a big bike ride and see if I can shake it off, sweat it out. But I dare not. Wednesday comes and I decide to ditch the 10-mile swim altogether. There's not much else I can do now; a couple of gentle swims in the lake or sea, no more than an hour at a time. Keep the exercises going, stay flexible; avoid injury, hangovers, contagiously ill people, and undercooked chicken. Check the weather forecasts. Stop checking the weather forecasts. No, keep checking them. Enjoy being on holiday, do some nice stuff with the kids, a couple of scenic walks, catch a movie or two. Eat. Eat some more. Top up on a few carbs here and there between meals. Devour some crisps – it's all part of the nutritional preparation.

But what if I'm not up to it? All these people have committed to a day on the boat, and I might just conk out half-way across. Surely it would be sensible just to call it off and avoid such a huge inconvenience for nothing? I know my team are spot on. I am the only unknown quantity in all of this. The weather is the least predictable factor, but at least it follows patterns and what it does is nobody's fault. I may just be rubbish and beg to get back on the boat after a couple of hours. I really should have kept this to myself – only told the people involved. There will be people on the slipway waiting for me to swim in to the beach, I can't hide it from them if I don't arrive.

Either I have to take my mind off it altogether, do unrelated stuff, or I have to focus on the positive actions. Continue to fine tune any aspect I can, aiming to increase chance of success and decrease chance of failure. I busy myself making the first prototype of my feed pole and basket, then meet Laura at the lake to test it out. What I don't do is any more research or reading of other people's experiences. Now is not the time to introduce any new ideas or spook myself with descriptions of hazards or difficulties. Fortunately, my friend Chris visits for a couple of days. We spend most of the time wandering about, diving in and out of cafes to dodge the rain and wind, not really experiencing Bristol at its best. I try not to make my swim the staple of our conversation; fortunately, he's an interesting bloke and we share a rich history of schooldays and motorbike adventures so there is always plenty of reminiscing to be done. It's not just swimming friends who are important, I feel both boosted and settled by his company. Perhaps just coincidental, but Chris went home, got his bicycle out of the garage and promptly did the biggest two-day ride of his life.

An unsettled climate and threats of low-pressure systems creeping in from the west become an increasing likelihood as the 2nd August nears. We head to my mum and dad's house for a couple of days for a bit of relaxation. I bore them senseless with constant updates on every source of weather forecast I can tap into. If there had been cows about I'd have been just as unhealthily obsessed with whether they were lying down or standing up. Physically, I am feeling better, tough enough to take the swim on, but definitely still not at my best. It is Monday. For logistical reasons, Wednesday is the best day for the swim (5:00am on the boat), Thursday and Friday are back-up days. Tuesday could happen at a push, but I'd be a vital crew member down and the tide timings would provide some additional awkwardness.

Of course, I am desperate to be presented with what I deem to be perfect conditions. But I must not forget that huge amounts of my preparation has been aimed at broadening the extents of the definition of 'perfect', I have done everything I could think of to be able to say, "That's good enough, this and that aren't quite what I'd hoped for, but I've got that and the other in place to deal with it – let's go!" Perfect? Let's revisit that too: we are not talking glassy smooth seas and still, warm air here. I have decided to take on the Bristol Channel because it has issues. I enjoy the sea, I like waves. I know I would not be happy sliding out onto the slipway having been the cause of the biggest ripples on the surface that day. Most of the time I look out at the channel it is posturing, puffing out its chest, blustering threats and flexing its pecs at anyone who thinks they're 'ard enough to 'ave a go! I don't want to sneak across its lawn while it's on holiday and the sweet old lady next door is popping in to feed the fish. I want to duck, dive, dodge and strut across its yard when it has unchained the dogs, kicked its boots off, settled into its rocker on the porch, shotgun across its lap, and a couple of home-brews under its belt. That is how I picture the channel, that is the one I want to cross.

The forecast looks bad. The low-pressure front from the south-west is lumbering in, squeezing its way up the channel between Devon and Wales and stomping heavily towards Bristol. Things look to get going around Tuesday, the breeze beginning to pluck at the surface of the estuary. By Wednesday morning it is expected to drag air in from the south, with threats of 40mph gusts building the swell above a metre and capping the peaks with white stuff. Thursday and Friday are expected to be Wednesday's feral cousins. This, in all likelihood, prohibits the swim for this window of tidal conditions. Paul will find it extremely difficult to effectively steer the boat at such low speed against the wind and the tide, and if he can't track a precise path, I definitely won't be able to. There is a slim chance the weather front will tame itself a bit before it arrives, and this is where I see a possible silver lining. If it became 60% of what it threatens to be, then Wednesday would suddenly become possible, with the conditions I crave, but Thursday and Friday would still be too rough. In this situation it would be all go for Wednesday and I wouldn't have to have an awkward conversation with my crew encouraging me to wait for smoother waters on one of the following days – because they won't deliver that.

But the forecast does not ease off. Monday night conversations with Steve and Paul are rightly decisive, and the decision is to wait a fortnight for the next three-day tidal opportunity. Steve has gone with his trusted method of studying the conditions near Lundy Island to get a feel for what's coming our way. Paul has seen these patterns many times before and can probably picture very clearly what the middle of the channel will be like, and it's no place for a swimmer. Bubbling about in the background is the "Sod it – I fancy a crack at it anyway!" bravado, but I suppress it and go with what my crew says. Of course I do, that's why an experienced team is far preferable to finding a mate with an old, borrowed dinghy. Bugger.

Thus begins, for me, another fortnight of limbo. The new potential dates are 16th, 17th or 18th August (Wednesday, Thursday, Friday again). I am only just beginning to wake up each day feeling near my physical best, so at least I have longer to get sorted, but I'm really not sure what to do with myself. Suspecting that postponement was a possibility we had steered clear of planning anything too definite as a family. Not quite knowing what you're doing is irritating on a personal level, but when you're the one stuffing up the plans for four other people, the guilt takes over. If it is delayed again, we end up with the next set of dates being right at the end of the summer holiday, when we are intending to be in Swanage for the week. This isn't the pressure I was anticipating. So much has to fall into place.

I know I am not alone in this frustration. These same climate variations are causing problems for the English Channel crossers who have slots booked this summer. It is impossible to swim regularly at Clevedon without running into people who are training for that iconic crossing. In particular, many of my swims this year have been brightened and energised by the presence of John Myatt and Donald McDonald. John is hoping to complete a two-way, two-man relay crossing later in the season, with his friend Mark Leighton in the water and Donald on the boat as support. I have seen first-hand the thoroughness of their preparation and their determination to succeed. They too will be well aware of the long-range forecasts.

I start the fortnight by getting myself down to the beach on the Wednesday afternoon at high water, when I would have been arriving on the slipway. Lurching about in the waves and seeing how hard they hit the beach is a lot of fun, but it does confirm that we had been wise to postpone. Thursday and Friday do exactly what it said on the tin. Right decision.

What do I do now with my training? Should I reschedule my 10-mile swim? I honestly don't feel like it: the waiting has increased the opportunity for mental demons to work their way in, and recalling the tedium of the previous long swims, I'm not sure that it will offer me any positive perspective on my swimming right now. Fourteen days doesn't seem long enough to ramp up the hours and then re-taper either. I chat with Laura; she suggests a few one-hour swims, two hours at most, just to stay 'topped up'. I have no idea if that is a good plan in physical terms, but it strikes a chord and I feel positive about it, so I schedule a few swims in. By the time I get to Monday, nine days to go, I'm ready to do a couple of hours but keen to avoid laps of the lake. Laura agrees to meet me at 7:00am, an hour before high water. We do a length of the lake, hop out into the sea, swim across the bay, under the pier and onto just past Ladye Bay. It's dull, grey, breezy and a little bit choppy. Perfect. Turn with the tide and head back to the lake. It's at least as good for my soul as it is for my shoulders.

I have a few days (at last) of feeling strong, positive and ready, but it is the external factors which cause the tension. The forecast is almost identical to last time. Possibly not as severe, and they don't seem quite so sure the wind will keep its ferocity as the weather system heads towards us. Jo McCready-Fallon cannot make the new date which leaves me a crew member down. Fortunately, I had already primed Gavin and a quick text message is all it takes to sort that one.

The forecast for Wednesday 16th is settling as it draws closer. Just like the last one, the wind builds and turns southerly through the day, but all the speeds are a few mph slower than before and a little less threatening. Thursday and Friday are predicted to ramp up the atmospheric energy and look the wrong side of the borderline. Phone conversations with Steve and Paul again, and the decision is it's Wednesday or another postponement. We agree to head for the boat on the Wednesday morning all systems go, but to be prepared for the overnight conditions to take the decision away from us again. Paul is positive, but clear that it is our intended early start which is rescuing us. It is apparent that I need to get over there and get on with it – the longer I am in the water, the tougher it is going to get as the wind picks up. Whilst there is still a threat of postponement, it looks as if I stand a decent chance of getting exactly the conditions I wanted. This is not quite such as neap a tide as the original dates, so the tidal stream is a little stronger and faster. Low water a little lower and high a little higher. This means a bit more negotiation of sandbanks at the start when the water is low, and a tougher fight across the central shipping lanes when the flows are fastest a few hours in. The basic plan remains the same though: swim across the tidal flow, aiming well south of my intended finish point, but let the flow bring me up the channel as I cross it.

Tuesday morning, the day before I hope to swim, I am at Clevedon Beach with two lads I have been coaching. This is the moment we find out if our sessions have been successful. They have gone from being nervous about getting into the lake and unsure of how to gauge the hazards of sea swimming, to planning and executing today's swim from Ladye Bay to the pier. They have trained, sorted the timings, researched the tides, monitored the conditions, put contingencies in place and arranged a land contact. I am just there to accompany them and stick my nose in if necessary. It goes well, the weather is favourable, and we sit in the sun afterwards to discuss what they might do with these new-found skills. It feels like a miniature graduation. It is also my chance to take a look across the estuary and visualise myself arriving here about this time the next day. Today, it is calmer than I would like. Being high water, the usual crowd of beach swimmers are here; a few of them know of my forthcoming exploits and come over to wish me luck. There are some experienced swimmers here and their positive and hearty encouragement is a welcome and timely boost. "I'll bet you're hoping for conditions like this?" features in almost every conversation. I'm not, but I keep that to myself.

Emerging from the water is a bearded gentleman, grinning as if the sea has refreshed parts other waters cannot reach. As he picks his way up the beach across the stones, I realise it is a recently retired work-colleague, Mark Finch. This is a man who oozes adventure and looks to embrace the richness of life in all its glory. We have, as always, a life-affirming chat. My swim is news to him and he is so thrilled to hear about it that I start to feel guilty about having been fairly selective and nervous about publicly revealing my plans. He has since told me a few stories of his sailing exploits in the Bristol Channel – tide and conditions playing havoc with his plans: I am very glad he kept them to himself today. Between us we figure out how his daughter can hunt down my progress for him tomorrow on social media, and he leaves me with the warmest of wishes and an energetic handshake.

Overall, my trip to the beach has been an ideal parry to the looming emotional haymaker of tomorrow. The afternoon is spent going over all the details, further fettling with the feed basket to make it a touch more robust, and a back-up bungee taped to the pole. I spend an hour or so in the kitchen carefully measuring scoops of maltodextrin, dextrose and ground oats. Lots of funnelling into bottles with added dashes of blackcurrant, a whole lot of shaking and coloured cable-ties secured round the bottle necks. The blender swiftly sorts the oat, banana and honey smoothie. Eggs are boiled, peeled and boxed and the list is duly ticked. That list is my world for a few hours until all the equipment is gathered and bagged, or boxed, ready to transport to the boat. I don't really remember the rest of the evening, but I suspect I failed to settle on any particular activity and spent a long time lying in bed wondering why I ever thought an early night was even worth trying. Sleep must have sneaked up on me at some point.

Chapter 5

THE DAY IS HERE

K nowing full well that there are two alarms set for 3:00am, I lie awake, glancing at the clock every few minutes. I've been doing this since 2:24am. Some more sleep would be welcome: I can't be sure what time I eventually calmed enough to sink into a night of unsettling dreams, but four hours of rest is probably on the optimistic side. By this point I have already got up, breakfasted and set off for Portishead Marina at least three times, each time having to turn back fretfully for some essential, forgotten item. During the final journey matters are complicated further by my growing need and desperate hunt for somewhere to urinate. In my dreams, I can find toilets everywhere, magic them up in the least likely of circumstances. Without fail though, they are never useable: locked doors, full of tomato plants, already occupied by B.A. Baracus, choir rehearsals for the acoustic properties of the tiles, a queue behind me creating insurmountable manxiety. Whatever the reason, I guess they all contribute to the building pressure in my bladder which eventually wrenches me from sleep. The panic eases in a few seconds as I assimilate the facts before me. Still dark. 2:24am. Jo still asleep next to me. Head de-fugging, I am not late for the boat, I have not had breakfast, the day has not yet started, this is not the disaster I have just been so convincingly and repeatedly suffering in my slumbered state.

No chance of getting back to sleep, my mind does what it does best and starts to work down the strong visual image of my kit checklist. It's the same as last time. I can't forget anything, it's either already in the van, in the hall (piled against the front door), or right at the front of the fridge. The fridge stuff will be remembered because the bags for it all are hung on the front door handle. It's all covered. Maybe just once more over the list though. No, focus on now. We sleep in the loft so it's easy to tune in to the sounds of the weather outside. I checked the wind forecast shortly before I went to bed, and it sounds as if the 12mph winds expected at the start of the day are duly up and about their business. Can't hear any rain.

The radio comes on at 3:00am, and I switch off the alarm on my phone just before it goes off. This is it now, the process begins. Wondering how long to leave it before ringing Laura, as promised, just in case her multiple alarms all somehow simultaneously fail, my phone buzzes its text alert. "It's ok, I'm up! See you soon!". I'm never one for leaping out of bed ready for action. Early mornings are not an issue, but getting properly perpendicular and fully functional is a paced and measured process; my body and brain take about an hour to get the party started. I know I need to get up now to arrive at the boat in an operable state, but nervousness is keeping me under the duvet. Getting out of bed is the point of no return. If I stay here, I could still believe I'm capable of this swim. If I get up, then I'm one step closer to possible failure and knowing, for sure, that I couldn't do it. On the fifth or sixth utterance of "right" last night's final cup of tea demands its last hurrah and off I head to find a useable loo. Jo, as reliable and tolerant as ever, is already on the move.

Poking my head round his door and peering into the dark, Jake looks comfortably out of it; he's a busy, growing lad and could do with every bit of sleep he can get. I feel guilty shaking him by the shoulder, but I need him today. We leave Stan and Eddie to their slumber and begin the cycle of bowls of porridge, cups of tea, fruit and nuts. Today, of all days, breakfast matters. I have it all planned, but it's all a little harder to swallow than usual. Jo moves, constantly; gathering stuff, checking things, making sure Jake and I are equipped for any emergency. Attempting, unsuccessfully, to conceal my grouchiness I don't bother with conversation, I am simply focussed on being out of the door on time, with everything I need. Jake has no doubt got his side of things covered but I probably irritate him with frequent checks.

Shortly before 4:30am I am staring into the boot of the van, scanning each bag and reminding myself what each item is for. Feed pole?, check; pump-action flask?, check; feed bottles?, check...... Once more back into the house, scan the inside of the fridge, turn slowly and scan the hall. There is nothing left in here, time to go. I am still nervous, but not about the swim itself: it is practicalities which niggle at me; parking, forgetting my earplugs, getting the wrong day, roadworks, one of my crew getting lost or breaking down en-route, the marina lock-gates failing to open. Aaagh! The van starts faultlessly and the roads are quiet though.

Crawling carefully over copious speed ramps, twisting through the maze of uniformly bland estate roads which serve the multiplicity of Portishead's harbourside flats, we eventually arrive and park up on the side of the road just a few hundred yards from the access gate to the marina boardwalks. It is, of course, dark, but the air is crisply fresh to the taste and unpolluted by noise. There are enough streetlights and harbour related illuminations to keep us functional. Once the van's tailgate has hissed its way up above my head, Jo, Jake and I grab two or three bags each and at just the right moment Laura appears to scoop up the last few things. We are the only sound and motion around, so were presumably quite easy to locate. A final scan of the boot to make sure we've got it all, pull the tailgate down, lock the van and make sure I give the keys to Jo. I need her on the beach in Clevedon later, so can't afford to strand her here. Ruby D will be easy to find in the mooring closest to the lock gates. As we shuffle towards the marina, there is a figure already there, staring out across the boats. Gavin. First to arrive. He grabs a bag and as we approach the gate, Paul has already spotted us, opened the gate and welcomes us down the ramp and around the boardwalk to the boat. Laura, Paul and I have previously whiled away a pint or so studying charts and talking through plans. Paul has met Jake before when we first came to look at the boat. Gavin and Jo introduce themselves to him and Jo is no doubt deciding if she trusts this man to keep me safe. This is an odd lull in the process for me. We are here in good time, with everything we need, but not much will happen until the lock gates open at 5:30am. My phone tells me that Steve is on his way, and although I know he has plenty of time, that is now the natural fixation for my jitters. He rings, he is somewhere along the edge of the marina, but not quite sure where we are. It's a very easy fix as we have a 20-foot pole adorned with three red lights directly above us. I think they change colour to indicate the status of the lock and gates. The rest of us are on board Ruby D, having carefully stepped over the rope Paul warned us about. Steve arrives, in plenty of time, and I can now ease myself off this particular heightened level of nervousness and take a small step down to the next one, save for a few seconds of angst as Steve takes a trip over the rope. Fortunately, a bit of deft footwork turns it into a jovial ice-breaker rather than an unfortunate jaw-breaker. Full house, so now where do I focus my fretting?

It seems that shuffling stuff about is a good thing for me to do right now, Jo has her camera out and Paul is fuelling the boat. It is getting closer and closer to the point where I only have to concentrate on the simplicity of swimming. All that's left for me to do is make sure I show Gav and Laura where everything is. All the feed bottles, the feed schedule, the spare powders and bottles if needed; the 5-litre pump-action flask already full of boiled water, the straps to secure it for the journey, the spare stopwatch, my spare hats and goggles, the painkillers; it is all there somewhere. No need for me to dish out a detailed brief for the crew on the day ahead: Steve will do that. I know this bunch, it will all be sorted. Just……… relax…….. until it's time to squeeze into my scrimps.

A few minutes still until we move. Paul is in radio contact with the harbourmaster to check the gate timings, the crew are fiddling about and chatting. I am staring at the back of the kitchen trailer up on the harbour walkway; the scene of many a happy bacon sandwich to punctuate big, social bike rides. Bacon, with a slice of black pudding – just part of the past few months' training regime! All sorts of big and little efforts have brought me to here and I can't help but feel smug as the quality of my team really begins to hit home. This bunch right by me on the boat all the way, and Jo, having got me here, will later be on the slipway with Stan and Eddie ready to hand me a mug of tea, towel, clothes and food. Momentarily thrilled, happy and excited. This really is it, but it begins to dawn on me that I might be the weak link in this otherwise robust chain. I am hit by a sensation which most probably refer to as butterflies in their stomach, except mine are pterodactyls engaged in some sort of fierce territorial battle. My heart skips a couple of beats then squeezes them back in a few seconds later. I grip the cold handrail of the boat, squeeze hard and focus on a few deep, steady breaths. The prehistoric creatures in my stomach seem to ease into a truce, just squawking at each other from a distance, and my pulse settles back to its usual bud-dum, bud-dum, bud-dum. My grin still needs a little forcing for a couple of group photographs, but the distraction is welcome. A year or so of work and waiting to get to this point and I'm worried the relatively short bit that's left is going to be more than I can handle. From invincible to incapable and back every few minutes, whilst nothing actually changes. I have about an hour of this ahead of me, perhaps the cruise across the channel to Penarth will mollify it a touch. Vastly experienced at this, Steve knows just what to say and gives me permission to be in whatever mood I need to be in; no need to make small-talk, no need to feel responsible for the crew. I can meditate or put on a show – whatever gets me through.

We chug backwards out of the mooring and do a little shimmy through the first set of gates. Paul pulls up alongside and secures the boat to the floating walkway inside the lock and it is time for a genuine sinking feeling. I experience some guilt at the sheer scale of the mechanical motion which is set off just for us. Massive pistons push the huge lock gates into position behind us and Jo strides across the top to get a few last photo's as we descend with the emptying water. The 8-metre drop is testament to the tidal range we are dealing with over the course of the swim and equates to around 3000 cubic metres of water flowing out of the lock to bring us down to the current sea level. Descending in the dark and looking upwards the sky still appears black beyond the lights above us, but the opening of the gates out to the estuary brings about a dramatic change as we look to the north-east. Avonmouth and Portbury docks might not make it onto many postcards, but as a skyline silhouette for the rising sun they have got it bang on this morning. Even the Second Severn Crossing is outlined clearly just along the bottom edge of the variegated, glowing strip of orange and pink. Most of the sky is populated with cloud, but little of it particularly heavy. It seems all the different types of lightweight, fast-moving clouds are holding a convention, but one or two of their well-nourished, thicker-set, elder brothers have sneaked in for the free buffet. The sun has surfaces galore to play with as it enjoys the narrow window of opportunity to throw its light from far across Gloucestershire and glance it off the underside of the clouds and the surface of the estuary. Vast warehouses, cranes and wind generators sharply throw shapes against the backdrop, relishing their moment of atypical glamour.

No doubt there are a couple of fishermen, a few runners, some cyclists, dog-walkers and the hard-working Pill Hobblers over at the docks all gazing at their own personal sunrise, but the full glory of this one is ours. Part way across the channel, tucked out of the breeze behind the cabin and staring back across our wake; nobody else has this vantage point, these colours, this splash and taste of spray, this motion of the boat, this reason for being here, these friends to share it with. Nobody has laid this on for us, we haven't jumped on a bandwagon and bought a ticket for this, there was no waiting by the computer with a credit card at the allotted time trying to sneak into a virtual queue along with hundreds of others. It was planning, consultation; generosity and wisdom of others; hard work, encouragement, patience, luck and nature's say-so: that's what has placed us here and made this our sunrise. It is so impressive that it overwhelms my concerns and I enjoy a good twenty minutes of simple appreciation. Perhaps it's some deeper sense of scale and perspective which, at some level, is rightly trivialising and negating my worries, putting me in my place. But I don't really think so. This is just a strikingly engaging arena in which to perform and I am too rapt in it to worry about stuff. Until I notice the time.

Jake and Laura are already posting some photographs of the sunrise on the social media group. Not many people are up yet, and those that are probably have more pressing things to do at 6:00am than check on my progress so responses are sparse at this point. Paul has assured us that there is good phone coverage across the route and the plan is to keep the updates flowing. We are very much hoping it will be a two-way process with messages of support reaching us out in the middle of the channel and communicated to me via whiteboards. (I have scattered lots of them about the story, even strategically positioned a few. Suffice it to say some considerate editorial control is exacted by the crew so not all of them make it as far as the whiteboards……..).

Leaning out over the siderails into the vigorous, fortifying rush of wind and spray it is easy to spot a rapidly approaching Cardiff. An intense glow with sparkling highlights, it fires a glistening beam of reflection straight at us across the estuary surface. It is not a clean ribbon of brightness, it glimmers and sparkles between shifting stripes of darkness: no polished veneer atop this sea. The look of the surface combined with the lurching, bouncing judder of the boat as it claps into the oncoming waves gifts me the broad brushstrokes as I paint the picture of what is ahead of me. Having seen a savage, angry sea bring waves thumping onto Clevedon sea front, crashing up the sea wall and over onto the road above, it is clear that this morning's sea is far from its moodiest, but I'm not convinced it got out of the right side of the bed either. We are in the middle of the channel where the biggest, strongest and fastest of everything comes together. Right now, the tide is still on its way out and the wind is here but smooth and steady, the sea is choppy. By the time I get back out here under my own steam, crossing the deep shipping lane, the tide will be flowing up the channel towards Gloucester and will have reached a speed of about 3mph. Having already blown straight up the channel overnight along the route of maximum fetch the wind will have created a bigger swell; right now, it is probably just leaving the North Devon coast and planning on meeting me back out here at about 10:00am. As suggested by the forecast, the wind is shifting around to come from the south and picking up speed. It will tumble over Brean Down, Weston and Sand Point and turbulently hit the waves side-on. My mid-channel destiny is coming into focus: the tide and the waves will be pushing me north-east, so I will have to swim towards the south-east and into the wind which adds a margin of extra effort to my normally very relaxed arm recovery: it's not much, but the tiniest bit of additional work for my shoulder muscles to stabilise my arm and push it forwards against the wind rather than just letting it fall may take a toll over twenty thousand strokes or so. Waves will be lifting and dropping me from my right which in isolation is not a problem for the mechanics of my swimming: I've practised and enjoyed much tougher stuff than this is likely to be, but I haven't done it with a stomach full of liquid feed before. My long practice swims to test my feeds were in the lake – some chop, but no swell. Swimming parallel to the waves plays havoc with body rotation so I can expect some unfamiliar stomach sloshing at the very least.

Engaging with the sea and assessing the conditions is doing me some good now though. I am eager to get on with it, keen to be tested. Pencils sharpened, calculator ready, last glance through revision cards done, invigilators just laying out the last few papers in the exam hall. Let me at it before it all falls out of my head. The general consensus is that it is time for me to spin around in soft focus, hollering "by the power of Neptune" over a bed of trumpet and Hammond organ, and emerge from the blur in my stretchy rubber hat and super-pants, prematurely triumphant and ready to save the world. It is a far, far more awkward process in reality. I am in comfy, all-over clobber, well layered up, enough clothes to fill a bin bag. What I intend to replace it with (hat, goggles, earplugs, trunks, sun-protection and petroleum jelly) all fits in one coat pocket. Madness. There is plenty of space out on the deck to change, but also wind, spray, a damp floor and not much to lean on, so I retreat to the hidey-hole in the front of the boat. There is a cushy, padded surface to sit on and plenty of space to spread my accoutrements around me. Sitting to change isn't easy and the ceiling above is low; with each thump of a wave I bounce upwards and risk a blunt thwack on the head. Each item of clothing requires a different arrangement of limbs and I have to chuck modesty straight out of the porthole. I bag my clothes so they are easily accessible for the crew: they are all baggy and easy to put on. With any luck, I won't see them again until I am at home, but if I'm fished out of the water in a bit of a state my crew may well have to dress me. Nobody wants that, but it must be prepared for. I would like to keep warm for as long as possible, but it's really only my head and feet I can keep covered at this stage as it is time to apply a bit of slap. I engineer my way back out through the cabin, past the warmly-clad crew, and onto the deck. I wouldn't bother with sunscreen today if I was wandering about on land in shorts and t-shirt, but I can't change my mind later in the swim, so on it goes. I clumsily slather it on all the bits I can reach but I need a bit of help across the back of my shoulders. All those hours doing flexibility exercises, but none of them quite gave me that kind of reach. A couple of baby-wipes to cleanse my hands, then it's latex gloves on and pot of petroleum jelly at the ready. No point being timid about this. Neck, front of shoulders, armpits, beneath any kind of paunchly over-hang and rubbed in thickly to every point of contact between seam and skin. Wriggle it all about and re-apply. Perhaps I should have soaked my trunks in the stuff overnight? I have to reach out to steady myself a few times as the boat rocks, leaving little blobs and smears of the stuff dotted around for the crew to discover later. I am almost ready, Paul is slowing the boat and we are approaching Penarth Pier. Steve begins to point out the slipway, the official start point, then suddenly we've stopped and everyone is out on deck. Laura's pointing her camera at me while Paul gets the ladder in place. It is time to steel myself, time to find my zone.

Self-belief is a clear asset at the start of any venture; it is crucial, at pivotal moments like this, to be able to look yourself up and down with a steady, critical eye and draw strength from what you see. Five minutes before I step off the boat I stand a proud six-foot-two, blue eyes, beach-blonde hair after a summer of salt and sun. Torso finely sculpted and shoulders sharply honed through months of training…….. all cruelly hidden beneath a flobbly layer of insulation carefully thickened over weeks of inflated dinners and endless bags of salt and vinegar crisps. Woolly hat pulled down tight, earplugs rammed in, rubber gloves snapped on, vassed-up moobs a-kimbo, pot-belly woppling about, butt-flubber bulging around the seams of budgie-smugglers with a sharp 80's graphic; more DeVito than Swayze. Dare to look down past withering, pasty white thighs above the sharp, jammer-wearer's tan-line, over knarly gnees to saggy socks wedged into old, sweaty trainers. Man, I am a water-god, I am stuff of legend!

At some point though, all this noble glamour must be put to one side and the unromantic, hard-boiled business of getting on with the swim has to commence. Gloves off, cap and goggles on. Some words of positive affirmation, wishes of luck, a couple of firm handshakes (so many reasons why hugs are out of the question) and I'm backing down the ladder into some of the least inviting water this beautiful country has to offer. I've been treated to a stunning sunrise of dense purples and pinks gently nudged aside by a varied and fascinating mixture of fulsome clouds slashed by scything wisps of pure white on a deepening blue canvas. Pressing up against the sky, the rising sun sharply highlights looming cliffs and curious pavilion architecture which anchors the pier to the shadowy, broad, stony beach. On the boat I have been surrounded by hearty encouragement, generosity of spirit and good humour. I am completely engulfed by the beauty of this world – apart from the bit I am lowering myself into. The water is some sort of brown. It is not warm, cosy cocoa. It is nowhere near a robust, earthy coffee. It is a million miles from smooth Belgian chocolate. Think rusty, turd-beige Austin Allegro dumped in a field of cattle for a couple of years; wipe it over with a dripping cloth and then wring it out into an old galvanised bucket. That's what is seeping through my narrow belt of technically advanced fabric and aggravating my sensitivities. I fear that I may just keep descending, the brown-ness will close over me with a sluuuurruup-plop and 47 years of largely misplaced effort will be reduced to little more than a fading ripple. Cold-water shock, however, has other ideas; the neuroendocrine response gives my kidneys a bit of a poke and I am "right back at-ya, estuary!" with a turbulent contribution of my own. The opportunity for a speech has slipped by and I am already busy formulating excuses; one minute in the water and I can't see me lasting more than half an hour – it is cold! Probably best to at least try though? The next five minutes is not flag-waving and fanfares before a well-wishing crowd, but more a scene from an Attenborough documentary illustrating how living organisms first clumsily slithered between sea and land.

"God Alec that water looks disgusting."

Tracy Williams

We are within an hour of low water, and there is not much of it left between me and the slipway. To reach land for the official start I swim a bit, then have to snake and crawl for fifty yards or so in shin-deep water. Walking is not an option for fear of losing a leg to the deep, ravenous mud, or breaking a toe and gashing my foot open on an angry rock. I cautiously feel and nurdle my way to the start point and turn to watch for the signal. A quick, regrettable glance down reveals my new frontage. I have been dipped in a thick, silty fondue and licked from head to toe by some hungry, barnacle-tongued, slobbering sea-hag. Never mind – she'll be gagging on petroleum jelly for the rest of the day.

Focus back towards the boat. A slight, nervous pause and the agreed start signal begins. There's some sort of noise and a

85

wave from Steve, but to be absolutely sure Gav breaks into a set of dance moves which have no place in a serious situation like this. Wriggling and giggling back across Hades' sunken rockery, the swim begins. This really is it. Time to get on with the job.

"Good Luck! See you on Clevedon Beach"

Lynette Blanchard

Breathing mostly to my right over the first minute or so I get to enjoy the sensation of movement relative to the solidity of Penarth Pier. This is not something I will experience again until approaching Clevedon and its pier almost 13 miles east of here. Penarth Pier is a heavy looking beast, vertical legs huddling closer to each other as they march towards the broader, bulkier, seaward end of the structure. To counter the conditions, the more exposed parts are thicker still, bolstered with concrete against crashing waves and screaming tides. It is low water, so a good 10 metres of height is visible, the density of the structure increased significantly by the multitude of cross-bracing between all the uprights. I don't pass close enough to touch the pier, but its bulk dominates the first couple of hundred metres of the swim. Although the necessity to swim from land to land means that this is a slipway to slipway swim, the close proximity of historic and well restored piers at both the start and finish cannot be ignored. This is a whoppingly proportioned pier to pier swim.

It will be at least half an hour before brain, limbs and lungs begin to co-operate and all the various energy distribution systems start to settle into a routine. Fortunately, I've done enough long swims in similar conditions to relax, knowing there is a period of synchronicity on its way. Rhythm does not come without a fight and a good deal of patience and concentration, but it will come. As the pier passes and fades behind my right shoulder the cold still jabs at my confidence.

Catching up with the boat is a more immediate concern though as Paul knows he has to drag me south of the sandbanks; Ruby D can operate in the shallows but grounding the boat would not help the day, and I need to head south at a good pace to set me up for crossing the shipping lane. Swimming with the boat is one major factor I have not practised before now, but I'm not trying to break any records and I've got a few hours ahead of me to get the hang of it. The plan is for me to keep the boat about 10 to 20 metres to my left. From where he sits behind the wheel and next to his navigation equipment, Paul can keep me in sight and guide me on the route which he and Steve will carefully engineer and adapt as the swim progresses. All I have to do is swim and feed. With the speed of the tide and strength of wind it isn't possible to steer Ruby D at my 2mph swim speed, so a distant game of leapfrog develops as I swim past the boat by 30 metres and Paul gently cruises back past me and on ahead to give me a clear target.

"Did you remember to warn the coastguard?"

Jeremy Murgatroyd

Rhythm is beginning to settle in and any sense of being cold has slipped away quietly. My stroke rate feels like it is somewhere around the "get on with it" mark and it's clearly sufficient to be generating some heat. I feel strong, I feel warm, I feel safe. Bullying muscles into doing their job is no longer required, my stroke is largely taking care of itself. I check in occasionally with various technique trigger points, look for familiar angles and try to sense my muscular responses; relaxed on recovery, triggering on catch and building pressure through the pull. Laura isn't waving any instructions at me and nothing hurts, it's all good. We are maybe a mile into the swim now and no longer in the calmer waters within the shelter of Lavernock Point. The channel is beginning to question my presence in its territory and raises its hackles. Conditions are not what most would consider perfect, but if I could have rung ahead with my order, this is exactly what I would have asked for. This is a sea swim. Calm water would be cheating. The previous two weeks have been stormy and there is already a 12mph southerly wind cutting across the tide. It promises to build in strength as the day goes on and come off the land from the south-east. It will prove to be a varied and exciting few hours with no two minutes being the same. I am enjoying the choppiness and the variable swell. It's high enough for me to bob in and out of view from the boat and on some strokes I get a satisfying grip on a hefty lump of water whilst on others my hand seems to slice momentarily through thin air. Breathe and be treated to a view across the sea from the top of the swell, breathe again and get sharply whumphed in the face as a collapsing wave decides it is time for a quick reminder of where I am and who is in charge. From the water I worry that conversation on the boat may turn to how these conditions might sap my speed, drain my energy and put the swim at risk. Although they will no doubt consult me, it is for the crew to make the decision to end the swim at any point, not mine. Happy as a pig in poo, but is that how it looks from the boat? No point dwelling on it, get on with the job. I reassure myself that a firmly stated "he'll swim in anything, this is the stuff he loves" from Laura or Gav would prevent it from becoming a discussion of note. Vital to have people in your support crew who know your swimming preferences and have experienced those conditions with you. But perhaps no such conversation takes place at all, how would I tell from here?

"Every stroke takes you further from Wales"

Jeremy Murgatroyd

Although the physical sensation of being out here tussling with the water is engaging, the visual experience is largely on the greyish-brown side of dull. Sea, boat and crew look pretty much the same throughout. Most of the change is above me as the blueness of the sky deepens between a surprising variety of cloud forms. Leaden, white, heavy, wispy, bulbous, dark and foreboding, light and fluffy; it all blows across at some point. I'm not sure if rain ever actually gets underway, but it feels as if I would probably have managed without the Riemmans P20 sunscreen slathered across my shoulders; I am definitely having to generate my own warmth. Curious about where I am and what more there may be to observe I try to indulge in a bit of sight-seeing. Waves have a habit of spoiling the view, so sight-glimpsing is the best I can hope for. The Holms are forward and slightly rightward of me with Flat to the left of Steep, but just overlapping; it will be a couple of miles before they swap position and I can get a sense of progress watching the gap between them gradually widen. To my left and a couple of hundred yards beyond the boat I catch sight of the Monkstone Lighthouse. Suddenly, the sense of this being a proper swim hits home and I feel I should soak it in. Treading water, I try to absorb the scale of the lighthouse and the peculiarity of looking at it from right here, right now, in a rubber hat and a pair of scuddies. I am only 15 miles from my house, but feeling a far more distant sense of remoteness. Plenty of people have taken in this view from a boat, but very few have swum here. This is peculiar to swimming adventures: on a bike, I don't think I could be this close to home and yet be somewhere that only a few other cyclists had ridden to.

"Get on with it!" shouts Laura, emphasising the point with the horizontal arm shoving action common to all competitive club coaches. To be fair, the tide has turned, and that pause has probably punted me 50 metres north of the carefully calculated line Steve and Paul are trying to tightrope me along. Better do as I'm told. And that's why I am chuffed that Laura is on the boat. Aside from her swim-coaching expertise and knowledge of my preparation, competence and limits, she has a feisty directness which scares me just enough to make sure I stay out of the decision-making arena and simply do as I am told!

"Alec was swimming at sea

With grease way up his knee

He had maldex and eggs

To make fuel for his legs

And warmed them with buckets of pee"

> *Written by Gavin on the boat and presented for me to read during a feed. It was also posted on the Facebook page as an invitation for others to have a go.*

Everything appears to have gone well in the planning so, once in the sea, I have very little to do other than a few thousand strokes, an occasional feed with accompanying gurgled "thank you!" to the crew; perhaps also a bodily function or two; maybe a smattering of bodily dysfunctions. Everything else, the whole shebang, is down to the crew. Consequently, I pass through periods of meditative tranquility, batches of boredom, moments of madness, and a few spells of speculation. I generally end up counting strokes; somewhere around the mid-300s I realise the pointlessness of it and stop. A few strokes later and it starts all over again. I try other things; song lyrics, favourite episodes of Father Ted, names of friends (doesn't last long), places I've been; but counting flushes in and takes over every time. Unfortunately, this is not sufficient to occupy my brain fully and when it doesn't have quite enough to do it wanders off into the dark woods, hunting out the eeriest looking, bramble-ridden paths. No biggy when sat at home on the sofa, but unhelpful almost to the point of self-sabotage during a hefty swim. Not easy to describe in written word, but this is about three minutes' worth.

"1, 2, breathe, 4, 5, breathe, 7, 8, breathe, dark, 11, light, 13, 14, breathe, 16, 17, wave! – gob shut, 19, 20, breeeeeeathe, dark, dark, bright, 25, 26, where's the boat?, 28, 29, breathe, 31, 32, still no boat, 34, 35, breathe, 37, 38, boat??, 40, 41, was (breathe) that Flat (43) Holm?, 44, boat behind me?, 46, 47, yes it was, 49, 50, look back – just waves, 52, 53, breathe, 55, 56, where the f(breathe)k's the boat?, 58, 59, breathe, 61, 62, look (pointlessly) forward, 64, 65, breathe, 67, 68, BOAT!!, thank **(70)** for (71) that, breathe, 73, 74, why the huddle?, 76, 77, breathe, 79, 80, what are they doing?, 82, 83, breathe, 85, 86, looks serious, just swim, just swim, breathe, 91, 92, what's wrong?, 94, 95, breathe, 97, 98, need (breathe) to see, 100, breathe, 102, still huddled, 104, why?, 106, breathe, 108, looking at chart?, 110, breathe, 112, I must be (breathe) way off (114) course, 115, just swim, breathe, 118, 119, still huddled, keep (121), going (122), breathe, 124, 125, they're (breathe) going to call it, 127, b(128)cks, breathe, 130, 131, drawing straws?, 133, who's the (134) doomsayer?, breathe, 136, 137, It'll be Steve, the Boss, Steve, breeeeeeathe, just (142) swim, just (143) swim, breathe, 145, 146, breathe, 148, 149, breathe, rhythm, 152, breathe, rhythm, 155, breathe, 157, 158, breathe, 160, 161, breathe, 163, 164, breathe………"

Then a moment later, crew un-huddled, everything looks normal on the boat again. I flollop on and try to remind myself it isn't my job to take on any of the swim-related thinking today. My crew have got everything covered. Pleasingly, despite this being the first time the group have been assembled as one unit, they seem to be enjoying their morning out on the boat. Paul and Steve have probably bonded over a chart or two; Gav and Jake know each other quite well from a couple of bike rides, swims and a bivvy at Sharrah Pool; Laura, Gav and Jake have all crossed paths in the lake or on the way to Ladye Bay. There is a shared interest in adventure, sport, the open water and, hopefully, a common goal on this particular day. I shouldn't need to bother myself with how things are on the boat, but I don't have a great deal else to think about so it's inevitable that I will be affected by what I see through my goggles. I am wearing my polarised ones, but their rose-tintedness fades in and out throughout the morning, occasionally being pushed aside by an encroaching vignette of dark, doubtful shadow. And herein lies a paradoxical quagmire for the swimmer's mind. I know Steve will have told the crew that they must look positive and be encouraging without fail, at all times. He's been there often enough to know that a swimmer only has to observe the tiniest of possible negatives such as a grumpy face, a shrug, a shake of the head or a punch-up and they will extrapolate the most cataclysmic of consequences. If the crew are sensitive to this and hence only display positivity, is it because things really are good, or is it because the dire truth is in need of a cover-up? And so what? As a swimmer, your only course of action is to swim as powerfully as you feel you can and take the feeds you're given. Soldier on regardless.

The crew are rocking, so everything's good.

Or is it?

Fortunately for me, despite a few private moments of wavering, my trust in the crew is high, so we each get on with our jobs and I mostly churn and chop away in contented solitude. With no lane ropes, no nearby points of reference, no clock to watch, it is surprisingly hard to monitor my own effort. I know my stroke count is generally 60 but I only have my own internal clock to judge that by. Laura and her stopwatch are keeping a close eye on, and recording, my stroke rate, so I can't deny that I slip off the pace every now and then. A couple of times I am aware that I have slowed; there is no tiredness or lack of energy, my muscles are responding well, my feeds are getting through; I have simply drifted off. My stroke is good enough to convince when I'm not paying attention to it, but it's considerably better and more productive when I am. Concentrating on the same thing for hour after hour is turning out to be a little trickier than I expected. Early in the swim, the first time Gav or Laura wield a "Push Hard" whiteboard I have a little submerged huff – "What do you think I'm doing? Do you think I haven't noticed I'm trying to swim a long way? I've got this, you know!". I wonder if an expansive, expletive-filled bubble breaks the surface differently from a normal exhale, perhaps a rare burst of blue in the sea of brown? And can they can tell from the boat? Upon the second bout of whiteboard-waving I realise how lacking in grace my previous reaction had been – "Oh, yes……. sorry! Interesting daydream, but got a couple of shoulders and arms to micro-manage. I'll get back to it straight away. Oops. Job in hand and all that……..".

"Morning.. .. keep swimming!"

Mary Stanley-Duke

"Good advice Mary!"

Stuart Summerell

93

This hastily scrawled ink on the A4 whiteboards is providing some welcome oomph. Detailed technique prompts (REACH, ROTATE), sophisticated motivational mantras (PUSH HARD!, GET ON WITH IT!) have their place and, let's be honest, give the crew something to do. More significantly though, they are my link to the gaggle of friends and (on the whole) well-wishers who are following my progress from land. Each time I feed I am treated to a volley of inspirational messages transcribed from phone screen to whiteboard. All heartfelt, many poetic, some evoking adventures past, a few humorous, and (you know who you are) a couple just plain rude. Without exception though, all uplifting. A bit of extra wind between my cheeks just when it is needed. There is a running theme though……. sorry for the distraction everyone!

"I know you're doing a little swim today Alec, but the real question is, am I actually going to be able to get any work done whilst following with excitement? ;) Swim Alec Swim!"

Vicky Bellamy

"I'm going to be late for work ... can't tear myself away Vicky. Lol!"

Jeremy Murgatroyd

"Yeah, having trouble getting started myself!"

Vicky Bellamy

"Officially your fault in getting no work done!!!! Keep going!!!! You're doing a fab job. Feel the sun on your back and take its warmth to power you on. Xx"

Mary Stanley-Duke

"None of us are getting any work done here!! Go, go Alec"

Helen Ball

Gratifying though it is to read something inspirational every half an hour, the essential purpose of these pauses is to feed. It needs to be quick as when I'm not swimming, I will go where the tide goes, which is not to Clevedon. In the first half of the swim, my pace needs to be sufficient to get me across the central shipping lanes before the speed of the tide picks up. Much too slow and I will end up in the Newport bound stream, which would be the end of the swim. Just a little bit too slow and I will be carried to Avonmouth; not necessarily a complete disaster but it would add a couple of hours to the overall time as I swim back down the coast with the then outgoing tide. Assuming I make it across the shipping lanes in good time the flow will still be strong and, ideally, I would like to maintain the requisite pace to directly hit the slipway. I would rather not wave at it as I drift past Clevedon to Ladye Bay, only to skulk back sheepishly a little later with the returning tide. Every pause for a feed will take me further up the channel, by as much as two metres for every second at the peak of the tide.

"Alec, think of it like the morning commute. Trust me it's better than the train and you get your own buffet car"

Chris Jones

Three figures at the railings and a long, yellow decorators' pole extended over the water with a plastic basket on the end. Time to eat. Yum. Overall, feeding from the water is a clumsy, artless process, though the first one passes smoothly whilst we are still in the shelter of Lavernock point; the water is relatively calm and the boat steady. Feed number two is a sharp learning experience; the waves are erratic and getting on for a metre high; the boat rocks, sending the basket high in the air then back down onto the water with a splash. I reach for the energy mixture to find the lid is still on the bottle. It's sorted quickly by the crew and then we learn it is too rough to rest the basket on the surface as the waves crash over and 'dilute' my feed.

After a couple of false grabs, I extract the bottle from the basket and the guzzling process begins. Treading water whilst being chucked about and trying to let the liquid flow quickly from the bottle straight to my stomach is unpleasantly difficult. The bottle seems to take an age to empty. Many swimmers favour bottles with very wide necks to speed this up, but I know I can't swallow the stuff that fast and would most likely just end up pouring it all over my face, so the control of narrower suits me better. Air goes down with the liquid, inevitably, and must come back out again while I'm still upright: try to start swimming without the burping process and it will bully its own way out a few strokes in, most likely bringing the feed with it. Returning the bottle to the basket feels like trying to do a jigsaw on a rollercoaster and consumes far too much time; too much drifting. However, job done, garble a quick but genuine "Thank you!" and back to the swimming. Over the next few minutes I have a couple of ideas to improve the next feed but can't communicate them to the crew. All is good at the third attempt though, as it seems they have come to the same conclusions. Gav holds the basket high above the water and I simply wait until a wave lifts me to reach it making an anticipated and controlled grab for the bottle. I do wonder if my proficiency at this will suffer as my shoulders tire. Bottle successfully in hand, guzzle slightly more proficiently than before then bypass the basket and simply lob it back on to the boat. Unfortunately (and I remain guilt-ridden to this day) the first one goes straight over the boat and out to sea. To ease my environmental conscience, I develop a better technique: leave a smidgen of liquid in the bottle to give the projectile some mass then aim for it to clobber an upright object on the boat and hence drop safely to the deck. It just so happens there is an easy to spot, bright pink target conveniently positioned at every feed.

From Laura to the Facebook group:

"He's keeping things humorous, he just threw a feed bottle at my head! I think it was revenge for messing up feed number 2."

A few feeds in, so at least a couple of hours have passed, and I become more aware of the wave motion. It's not because of the direct impact it is having on me, pitching and rolling me about. I don't have a great sense of balance at the best of times. Skateboards slip straight out from under me, rollerblades are simply treachery disguised as footwear and ice skating a complete waste of time. "You'll get the hang of it if you just give it a try, and it'll be loads of fun!" says everyone who has ever tried to talk me into a trip to an ice rink. Well why don't I take them to a cold, wet car park and spend an hour chasing them round, shoving them hard onto the ground every couple of minutes? After the trip to A&E for a couple of wrist and elbow X-rays we'll review that word "fun" shall we? Back to the point, my internal gyroscope spins well enough to keep me upright most of the time, but I don't think I'm overly sensitive to any movement I may do around it – seasickness is not an issue for me on a boat or immersed in the waves and I am confident that goes hand in hand with a poor sense of balance. So it isn't my own lurching which has brought the waves to my attention, it's the astonishing diversity in the views I get each time I breathe. Sky, bottom of a wave, boat way above me, boat nowhere in sight, a clear view of Flat Holm and Steep Holm with a bit of coastline behind, another wall of brown. On one occasion I even slap myself in the face with the back of my own hand as I slip down the back of a wave and hit the bottom of the trough a bit hard. Snatched glances of the Holms do confirm that I am somewhere out in the middle now; they have readjusted their relative positions to the way round I am used to seeing from Clevedon and a gap has opened up between them. Steve calls me in to the boat. He points to something in the distance which I cannot see, but makes it very clear that I need to swim hard towards it for the next half an hour. I get the gist though, we are aiming even more towards the south, which must translate to being in the fastest part of the channel now and the inherent need to avoid being dragged north. The rougher sea has not gone unnoticed on the boat either and Steve is keen to let me know that this is just a patch: I will be through it and into calmer waters in a few hundred yards.

"Just popping in the lake Alec Richardson... I'll swim a few lengths with you in spirit...xx"

Mary Stanley-Duke

Variety, they say, is the spice of life. They are wrong, it is smoked paprika, but they do have a point. This phasic nature of the swim is batting boredom firmly out of the park. Switching slightly away from being parallel to the waves they are still coming at me from my right, but also from slightly in front of me. This is fun, and a lot like some of the rough trips I've done between Ladye Bay and Clevedon Pier. Instinctively, breathing away from the wave direction seems smart and I have frequently overheard this wisdom being shared among open water swimmers. In light, high frequency chop I would agree, but in these conditions I find it far better to breathe mostly to my right, towards the splurging rollers. There is a sweet-spot to be enjoyed by timing my breathing on the top of a wave, giving a good view of the next one. Using a straighter-armed stroke, pressing down more at the front with my left hand to lift my head a bit higher, I can get a clear view forwards and take a good deep breath as I turn my head back to the right, having already cleared the peak of the wave and any white-water frolicking at its leading edge. My stroke changes above water too, right arm pitching over with more of a straight-arm swing a little bit like a one-sided butterfly stroke, pitching my momentum down the back-slope of the wave and shoving myself forwards with my immersed left arm knowing it's deep in the less turbulent water. Pull with the right and recover the left, but two strokes is just too short for the frequency of the peaks, so I momentarily pause and glide (not something I would normally encourage) with my left arm extended and right hand down by my hip, slipping up the forward slope of the next wave. Just as I feel my torso start to level out towards the crest, I push down again with my left hand to sight and breathe and repeat the cycle. It's a satisfying rhythm and feels like an effective way to work with the conditions: confirmed a few times when my timing goes awry, pitching me against the wave energy, losing me a breath and a morsel of momentum. Occasionally, when the timing is wrong, I look up too early at an advancing slapper of a wave: I forgo the breath and get my face back in quickly (it is contact with the surface of water which hurts, so best to do it under your own control), knowing from my training I can easily go another few strokes without a breath if I need to. The consequential reduction in stroke rate from timing it with the wave cycles will not have escaped Laura's notice, but it hopefully still looks purposeful enough not to raise any concerns. Keeping an eye on the boat is problematic as I am placing myself in the bottom of a trough at the very point my stroke would normally allow me to breathe to the left. Every fourth crest or so I have to sacrifice a breath, stick with the forward glance, but then whip my head to the left instead of the right and hope to catch a glimpse of Ruby D before my over-swinging right arm lands and drags my head back into the murk. Of course, this adapted stroke does not work as consistently and reliably as my description may suggest. A hit rate of 70 percent would be fair; the waves are not travelling in perfect lines of constant height and one in five peaks or troughs throws me off rhythm, saps my speed and leaves me stranded until I can regain it by throwing myself down the back of the next wave. It's true that the invention of this technique is borne of necessity, but I have not waited until now, half-way through this big swim to go through the whole "experiment, test, improve and repeat" cycle of invention. I have practised this many, many times before on my way along the Clevedon coast. On a calm day, I tend to swim a direct route, sighting on a distant feature and doing my best to head straight for it. On a rough day I will zig-zag my way along the edge of the channel; pitching myself directly into the waves for a few minutes, then cutting back across them or trying to hold a parallel path. My comfort with these conditions out here in the shipping lane is because coping with this was an anticipated necessity. I did my inventing of a rough-water stroke a while ago and left myself plenty of time to work through a few duff prototypes before stowing it in my armoury. There may be better ways of dealing with these conditions, but at this stage in my swimming development, this is the one I've got.

"There was a young man from Backwell

Who dealt with the big channel swell

He swam like a shark

and was back before dark

and now there's a legend to tell."

Mac Elliott

100

Increased awareness of the view to my right is a by-product of the crest-hopping. Though I hope very much that I am travelling east, or just north of east, I am distinctly aware I am still aiming for Worlebury Hill, overlooking Weston, which is definitely to the south-east. There are heavier clouds there which appear not to be moving, but the wind in my face strongly suggests that it's because they are headed straight at us. Looking directly to my right I must therefore be staring straight down the shipping lane. Paul will have contacted the Bristol Vessel Traffic Service at Avonmouth, so presumably he knows about the sodding great lump of steel and paint blocking itself onto the horizon. Some sort of cargo ship, but the view straight on to its bow is just a hulking rectangle, large enough to have a couple of cranes on deck. Worry not, worry not. Maybe that's why the last couple of whiteboard messages suggested that I should be keeping the pace up? This is a terrible time to have nothing important to think about. Of course, the crew are keeping me safe and even if by some terrible miscalculation we end up too near this thing they will have me out of the water and we will speed to safety in ample time. Unfortunately, an unwelcome, bursting boil of a memory pops into my consciousness. It was an article about the death of the aviator Amy Johnson. Details are not surfacing, but I recall that it was the Thames Estuary into which she had bailed out of her 'plane. A crew member from a naval vessel lost his life after entering the water in a rescue attempt and her body was never recovered. Putting the heebie-jeebies up me right now, in the apparent path of this big beast, is the main thrust of the article proposing that she had been caught up in the propellers of the very ship attempting the rescue. I have no idea exactly what kind of flow, turbulence, wake or whirlpools may occur directly around a huge thing like this, but I am confident I don't want to be near it. Just keeping on swimming does the job though, as a few minutes later the ship is well behind me, easily visible with the sun lighting up its side. Predominantly white with a rusty orange lower third, maybe two hundred metres long and thirty metres high; an enormous slab of brightness spanning between the mulch of the sea and the leaden weight of the perma-cloud over Wales. Just a short pause to take it in, and off we go again.

From the boat to the Facebook group:

"Going very well, looking like we could be coming into Clevedon earlier than midday. We'll keep you informed."

"Goodness, quick swimming!!! Nancy Farmer; get your swimsuit packed, looks like we're on for an earlier dip!"

Vicky Bellamy

Having not had any real sense of immediate progress since watching Penarth Pier slip past and shrink behind me, I am treated to a humbling reality shock as I encounter one of the shipping lane marker buoys. The roughness has settled a little, just as Steve said it would, and I get a better view of my surroundings with each breath whilst easing back into a more consistent, classic stroke. I know that the tide is moving me, but I cannot feel it. I am sure that, relative to the water around me, my stroke is pulling me in the direction I am pointing. I have to trust that the resultant motion of these two is taking me closer to my destination. I can see the coast ahead of me and sight what I think is Sand Point, six miles south-west of where I'm hoping to finish. Flat Holm and Steep Holm are where I would expect them to be. They are all distant so as points of reference for my immediate progress they are of little help. The boat is close by, but it's moving too, and not at constant speed. I need something which is of fixed position and close enough for me to observe my relative motion between each breath or two. Breathing to the left I spot the buoy, maybe twenty metres away at 45 degrees in-front on my left. Sticking to my rhythm, six strokes later I am breathing to my left again, subconsciously expecting the buoy's motion to be on a path parallel to the alignment of my body – it should still be distant and on my left, but just not quite so far in front of me. It simply isn't there. Three more strokes and I am breathing to my right – there it is – almost directly in front of me, just slightly to the right. Disturbingly, I appear to be no closer to it. Six more strokes and it is further to my right and shrinking fast but still, I am sure, in front of me. I don't see it again. Out there in the middle of the channel I have just enough wit about me to establish that my path relative to the buoy is directly perpendicular to the line between my head and toes. I teach relative and resultant velocity to A-Level students as part of my day job; a triangle of velocities on my whiteboard holds no fear for me. I can picture this triangle clearly in my head, the maths is simple, but it was brutally illustrated. If I made no progress towards the buoy, am I making progress towards Clevedon?

"Keep going Alec. Every stroke gets you closer to Clevedon."

Lynette Blanchard

Right now, I'm not so sure, but as nobody is telling me to get back on the boat, I have to trust that I am.

"Keep going. Pain is temporary, and glory is for ever, etc. etc...."

James Bevis

Unnerving bumps from below; salacious, slightly scratchy, body-length caresses from patches of floating seaweed; the slobberiness of a jellyfish encounter, which may transpire to be seaweed after all; the chance of a harsher impact with a lump of driftwood. These are all threats in stealth mode: unless a portion of the encountered object is above the water, or it hits me right in the eyes, I will only feel it and not see it. This adds some sort of edge to the swim, exhilarating and perturbing in equal measure. I have swum amongst jellyfish in the Mediterranean, in a clear sea. Mostly they were barrels hovering about in the upper couple of metres of the water. Slow-moving and clearly visible from a good few metres, they still had the uncanny knack of jumping out in front of me as if from nowhere. This really disturbed my rhythm as I found myself tilting my head back to look further forward, and not pulling on the breathing strokes until I was eyes-front once more. Gav was with me on that occasion and our target was a wreck just beneath the surface about 300 metres out from the beach. We found it, swam over it and stared down into the dark holes and shadows. Spooked, we turned and swam back to the beach as fast as our jelly-radar would let us. There is no visibility here in this thick, silty, brown fog and it is a little more relaxing for it. Guarding against what cannot be seen is a waste of effort and nervous energy, there is little choice but to swim with the freedom of assuming there is nothing to encounter. Each unexpected contact does elicit a shock response, but it doesn't have the hideous rapid build-up of anticipatory dread which comes with seeing the moment before impact. I do shudder at the same time my brain tries to rapidly translate the tactile signals into some sort of rational identification and hence assess any need for further panic. The fishy bumps are the oddest ones: I'm not sure what kind of creature would wish to investigate a brute this large disturbing the surface. Perhaps it is the opening move of a mermaid's courting dance, but this is not an area of social etiquette I have studied and, regrettably, I may have left a broken heart or two behind me in the channel.

Communication with the crew was discussed on the cruise over to Penarth. My main concerns were knowing when it was time to feed, and how I might be told if the swim needed to be stopped. The very embodiment of faithful, my five-year-old, £30, waterproof Timex watch has been on every swim with me;

pool, river, sea and lake. It does every working day with me too, only resting when I rest. But today it has a day off, nestled comfortably in my kit bag. I have decided to let the feed schedule be my only tangible clue to the time; it is another way of affirming absolute control to the crew. A two-armed wave, as agreed, signals to direct my attention to the boat and head in to find out what's up. It's a feed if the basket is being offered, instructions or questions will be shouted, written on a whiteboard, or both. Where necessary, I repeat an instruction back. Ears full of silicone putty make this a shouty process, but I don't think we're bothering the neighbours. The universal thumbs up serves its purpose on occasion too. If it's time for me to get back on the boat, then that is a simple instruction and the reasons can be discussed later. Should I be in no fit state to understand or follow the instruction then if they can safely fish me out, they will; a choice of four strong swimmers and a lifebuoy. If it is clear that I will resist and endanger any member of the crew, then it will be a lifebuoy on its own. Paul, of course, can radio the coastguard at any point. The very sad death of a swimmer in the English Channel just a week before gave this conversation all the gravity and respect it deserved.

Thus far, and I'm not entirely clear just how thus or far that is, the communication has been just fine from my perspective. For all I know, Laura, Gav and Steve may well be deep in discontented mutterings, bemoaning my misinterpretation and disobedience; but I don't think so. I have a reasonable recollection of my feed schedule so I have not yet been taken completely by surprise – an unexpected half a boiled egg should be well within my coping range though. Most importantly I am excitedly confident that there's another bottle of warm tea on the way soon. All the bottles so far have had a bit of warmth, presumably the premixed dose is being topped up with a dash of hot water from the flask. A proper cup of tea though....... bliss on a stick! I am slightly confused about

105

exactly how many feeds there have been and hence how long I've been swimming for. It's the same thing which catches me out counting lengths in the pool: the number in my head has been there so long, I've forgotten if it's the one just passed, or the next one still to come. Never mind, swim on. I have no distance markers, and the coast I am aiming for still just looks a long, long way away, much as it has done for the last couple of hours. If I've done six or seven feeds then I'm three or three and a half hours in, which could be anywhere between one third to two thirds of the way through. No doubt about one thing though – I cannot yet see Clevedon Pier.

"Just looking out of my window Alec, can't quite see you yet.... keep swimming..."

Rachel Pinnington

An hour or two pass with minimal fuss. Feeding goes smoothly and I am appreciating the test runs I did in the lake. The maltodextrin mix is sloshy and I suspect does not give my digestive juices much to get stuck into. I have no doubt that the oat, banana and honey mix is what rescues me from nausea. Half a boiled egg is not an appetising treat, but it is dense enough to fool me into thinking I've taken on some solids, despite pretty much having liquidised it between my teeth before attempting to swallow it. Ibuprofen slips down easy, taken prophylactically in anticipation of a shoulder twinge or two. There is just one previously untried item on my feed schedule and, if jelly babies could speak, they would have squeaked "You should have tested us out in the lake!" as I spit them back out and send them on their own maritime adventure. Prompts to get a move on feature regularly, suggesting there is still a danger of slipping off course with the tide. Land-launched quotes continue to provide a bit of a boost too. Waves still do their thing and pitch me about; mostly I still slip over them right shoulder first, but they are becoming more irregular in tempo and magnitude, and overall a touch calmer. Having already swum for a good few hours, this very much feels like a spell of business as usual. I can feel that I am tiring, my muscles have been on the go for a while now and it is not as easy to build steady pressure through my pull. Part weakening of the driving muscles, part blunting of the fine motor control; greater concentration is required to keep my rotation and guide my hand entry. No concern here, this is as expected. Better than expected. Only five weeks ago, six miles in the calm and relatively warm marine lake had put me in a much worse state than this. Three hours of swimming and testing feeds, the final mile ground its way into my bones, the monotony taking its toll in so many ways. My feeds weren't refined correctly at that point and I'm sure that was significant. Right now, I feel very much in control and with plenty in the pan but, unsurprisingly, a little less heat in the sauce.

Slightly worrying conversation in the Facebook group between Clare Mactaggart and Stuart Summerell:

"Alec! I can see you out of my bedroom window!! Well, not you yet, the boat. With my telescope. And someone in the back with an orange coat - Laura? So exciting!"

"Ah - please alter your course! You have now disappeared behind a giant tree in Herbert Park. If you would be so kind as to head a little further south, I'll get you back in my sights. Thank you."

"In your sights!!!! Do you have a sniper's rifle?"

"Yeah. My aim's not that great though, so I'll probably wait until he gets a little closer before I have a pop at him."

Visual clues, delivered in snatched glances of vaguely recognisable landmarks, begin to hint that the final stretch may be about to begin. I think I can pick out Wain's Hill and Church Hill to the south of Clevedon, above the marine lake, and the building covered slopes of Dial Hill forming the northern bulk of the town. I still cannot spot the pier, but I know roughly where it is along the vista. Just to the right of Wain's Hill, on the very southern edge of Clevedon there are a couple of transmission masts which fade in and out of view against the variable, cloudy backdrop. From this distance, I still can't judge my angle of approach. Sneaking in from the south, with a little assistance from the last couple of hours of the incoming tide, would be my approach of choice, but I think I would be nearer to Sand Point, Woodspring Bay and the sandbanks of the Langstone Grounds than I appear to be. Midday must be hereabouts and the last forecast I looked at this morning foretold a variable wind with peaks of 20mph about now. Bang on. Being closer to shore and in the shelter of a succession of headlands further down the coast, the swell has had its energy sapped, but the wind is capping what is left with slappy little upstarts. There is no rhythm to be had here and the going begins to get tough.

> *"There's cake at the finish and a pint ... keep going just one arm in front of the other xxx"*
>
> *Charlie Stockford*

Years of following my kids struggling up hills on bike rides comes back to bite me. They all dance ahead these days and impolitely wait for me at the top, but there was a time when they needed encouragement from behind. The exact phrases used elude me now, but the majority had the words "mental strength" in there somewhere, and I probably delivered these messages with the arrogance of one who felt they had it mastered. Splashing my way across the estuary, I am not completely losing it, but having mostly embraced my lack of control over the swim so far today, it is now causing me to experience humbling levels of anxiety. Map, I want to look at a map. I want to know exactly where I am. I want these irritating little jack-in-a-box waves to bugger off and find someone else to bother. I am done with seaweed, especially the bits which keep lodging themselves between my fingers. A bacon sandwich. If I had a kingdom to offer; a bacon sandwich would seem like a fair trade. I need a pee, I really, really, really need a pee. There has been no problem with this until now. Urinating whilst swimming is another of the techniques I have fine-tuned over the last few years; the skill is in triggering the initial relaxation and temporarily switching off my core, dragging my legs a bit, and counting. My record? Thirty-four strokes. Right now though, I am too anxious, too tense to start the flow. No disasters are apparent, no cloud of doom tracks me, but all the little things are coalescing into a ball of worry in the pit of my stomach, a black hole feeding hungrily on positive vibes, an energy sponge. Mental strength. My body is not letting me down, but my brain has dropped the ball. I am making up the conditions around me, adorning them with all sorts of perceived difficulties which may be there, but I am well able to cope with. I need to get back to the simplicity of the job: it's just some water, a couple of waves, a well-practised bank of strokes to focus on and a boat to keep in sight. Simple. This is not a struggle, not difficult. I am creating my own obstacles, and I know it.

"A river cuts through a rock not because of its power, but because of its persistence."

Emma Thomas

Real struggles are not an alien concept. Everyone is fighting a battle of some sort, and now is the time for me to remind myself of how much strength I have seen over the past few years from others in the face of devastating, life changing circumstances. Perspective. I believe in personal heroes, people we are close to who hold on to their standards in a consistent, unfailing way. Never a bad word to say about anyone. In constant pain, but more concerned about the comfort of their guests. Unfailingly positive in exceptionally negative situations which are not of their making. Right here, right now, what would they say to me? It should be, "Get on with it you whinging git, you chose to do this, it's your own fault, you're creating your own issues. Stop being pathetic about your imagined difficulties and man-up." But I know these people would be far more gracious and say something more like this, "Keep going, you've got this, you've done a great job already, you know what to do!" There is no enjoyment in this thought process, but there is positivity. I know I need to get back to the simple concentration of counting and rhythm, but numbers on their own are not enough to wrench me out of the doldrums and back to somewhere I can focus properly. A rope ladder, unravelling itself down the side of the well, comes in the form of memories of my personal heroes. I can do what I've trained to do, and that is my best chance of success. Landmarks on the coastline are getting clearer and so is my focus.

> *"About 20 mins ago I looked across the sea to sort of where you might be swimming and visualised one arm over the other. You know the drill, keep on swimming!"*
>
> *Vicky Bellamy*

Ruby D drifted behind me a few moments ago, and in the natural rhythm of the last few hours I expect to see her gently saunter by on my left again very soon. Engine noise hits me before the boat comes into view, much louder than I have been used to. The same, consistent distance away, but on my right now with the wind carrying the noise and a hint of fumes towards me. I can see the crew, but there are no messages and no waving, so I assume this is an adjustment of strategy rather than a significant change of plan. From the number of feeds I've had I know there is still an hour or more of tide flowing up the channel and potentially dragging me beyond Clevedon. The masts have not disappeared behind Wain's Hill, so I can deduce that I am still south of my intended landing point, but they've still got me pointing way back down the coast, counteracting some of the tide effect. My assumption is that Steve and Paul want to drag me further south still and that is easiest for Paul to switch to my right and gradually open the gap between me and the boat such that I get the hint and close it again as I swim. In conversation weeks ago, Paul had said that steering me by 'pushing' was undesirable as if I didn't take the hint then he could only re-establish a safe gap between me and the boat by turning the back of the boat, and hence the propellers, towards me. Maybe fifteen minutes of this go by, then Paul manoeuvres back to my left and it is apparently time for a feed. Buoyed by the unusual sensation of the coast getting closer as I swim, my little dip into negativity seems to have passed and treading water to feed is exactly the opportunity I need for relief. Laura probably attributes the length of this feed to tiredness, but the extra seconds are being used to relax all the necessary valves and offload some pressure. 200ml of liquid flow in, considerably more flow out. It does not escape my notice that I drift considerably during this feed, but it is time well spent as I feel a bit of fight coming back. The pier is just about visible now, so I know exactly where I am and where my landing point is. The side-on view of the pier means I have not yet been dragged too far north, but there is a sense of urgency creeping under my skin.

> *You may need to read Appendix H to get the kebab reference here.....*

"Final push now Mr Richardson. Enjoy imagining me gifting the kebab on a bus one night! Legendary well done. One stroke after another, just keep moving."

Pete White

111

I suspect Steve and I are having similar thoughts. We both know how this last patch of water will behave as it is around this time of the tide we can be found frolicking in the bay, trying to get around the pier or to Ladye Bay and back. Close enough to the landmarks to establish I am pretty much due west of the slipway, and I estimate still over a mile out. Choice one – turn more towards my endpoint and fight the tide a bit less; swim hard and give the flow less time to push me too far beyond the slipway and the pier, then stick close to the rocks, fighting my way back down the coast and under the pier to the beach against the tide when and where it is slower. Choice two – maintain a swim direction which negates the effects of the tide, but only leaves a small component of my 'forward' swimming motion to crawl sideways, crab-like, but on a direct easterly path to hit the slipway. A reception committee will be on the beach and I'd like to make as classy an arrival as I can: it has to be choice two. I can bin out and go for the first choice at any time, but a target is what I need right now. "See those masts? Swim hard for those, just beyond Wain's Hill – nearly there!", Steve and I appear to agree. I doubt I would believe what I am hearing though, if I had not forced myself to experience this kind of tracking in previous swims. Usually when the tide is heading the other way, having gone around the end of the pier on the way back from Ladye Bay on a spring tide, the only way to bring yourself directly back to the beach is to try to follow a path parallel to the pier. Should someone treading the boards of the pier choose to look down, they would assume that you are trying to swim straight under the pier, back up the coast, and failing. Should they be patient enough and watch for a few seconds they would notice the almost sideways movement along the pier towards the beach. The pier is about 300m long. I am now faced with the prospect of creeping sideways for about six or seven times that.

"Last push Alec Richardson you got this nailed!"

Helen Ball

Feeling the love again, excited by the prospect of finishing, my concentration returns, bringing a bucket full of resolve with it. I have two targets, one in front of me to point myself at, and one way off to my left to shuffle towards. Calmness has settled over the water with the shelter of land so I can sight more reliably. As I edge towards the beach, the masts will disappear behind the hills and I will need to continually choose new landmarks to align myself with, each one a bit further left than the last. Blackstone Rocks, Wain's Hill, Church Hill, the Pumphouse at the far end of the Marine lake, The Salthouse Pub, the bandstand then the slipway itself at the very last moment. Hopefully, with each breath to the left I will see my destination drawing me in. A surprising, and flattering, number of people intimated that they would try to be on the beach for the finish. High water brings its own little crowd as the regulars gather for their daily dip, but the speed of the flow suggests I am an hour or more too early to mix it up with them in the last few yards. When asked how long I thought it would take me I generally replied about 7 hours, suggesting my arrival would be between 1:00pm and 2:00pm. It really isn't my problem right now, but it feels like I may catch a few people on the hop. Jake has no doubt kept Jo and any other followers updated, so I think I can rely on a towel and some clothes being on hand. Arriving on home ground is beginning to add a little pressure, but in a really positive and inspiring way. There is a semblance of a gaggle of bodies somewhere in my intermittent glimpses of the beach; possibly just an assortment of strangers, this is Clevedon Beach on a reasonable day in the summer holidays after all. Regardless, the possibility of any spectators at all, casual or engaged, piles on the pressure of hitting the slipway straight on. Perfect endings are rarely an option, the joy of this one should be that I arrive somewhere I know, to see people I know and exit the water without having to swim back to the boat. Sadly, it means I don't get to celebrate immediately and directly with the crew, as they will head back to Portishead Marina without me. But overall, this feels good, maybe better than crawling out alone onto an unfamiliar bit of coast and only having a distant boat to wave to as a celebration.

From the beach, via the Facebook group, about half an hour before I finish:

"Think we've spotted you, are you about 1/2m straight out from the pier?"

Rachael Davis

"Plenty of standing around, when's the action starting?"

Gavin Price

"Not a spectator sport is it Gav?"

Jeremy Murgatroyd

Eeking towards the slipway is slow, but eek I do. Wain's Hill is in the crosshairs and I can make out the shape of the sea wall hemming in the Marine Lake. There are definitely figures somewhere near the slipway end of the beach, suspiciously gathered. Doubts have stalked me along the way today, never really getting a firm hold, but definitely having their dirty few moments with my vulnerable ego. They are well and truly quashed now, impotent and invisible behind my clear and tangible view of the end, which is at last in sight. I am done, I will make it from here, but I am desperate to do it staying this side of the pier, in sight of the beach. The boat is a lesser part of my focus now, but still a hugely reassuring presence. Jake should be getting ready to hurl himself in soon, though for all I know he's spent the last couple of hours being sea-sick and may be in no fit state. Someone, I am sure, will appear alongside me at some point, but I still can't gauge my true distance from here at water level so mustn't get my hopes up too soon. Gav is waving the feed pole over the side of the boat, seems about right, but I take a few strokes to think about it. Stopping now will drift me a good way off my beeline, possibly pitching me beyond the line of the pier. The last few minutes I feel as if I have picked up my pace comfortably with no sense of lethargy. Feeding has gone well and my muscles do not feel tired. Stuff it. Just keep swimming. Some sort of combination of arm wave and head shake is attempted whilst trying to keep rhythm and momentum and it appears Gav understands. I am acutely aware that Laura and Steve may have their own view on this with their superior view of where I am and what is likely ahead of me, so if the boat comes closer and further instructions are given then I will go with that. Whatever it is we all think we've agreed on though, it does seem that they are letting me crack on.

"Go Man Go"

Mum and Dad

Everything is going up; higher stroke rate (I think), better mood, speed of thinking, scope of thoughts, pool of energy, sense of urgency, likelihood of success. I am not sure if there is a swimming equivalent of limping over the finish line, but I won't be doing it regardless. If I don't finish strong, I won't land on this pass and will have to finish on the tide's terms rather than my own. In the absence of an aerial shot, protractor and a touch of trigonometry, I can't be sure of the exact proportions, but I feel as if less than half of my energy is taking me directly to the slipway. The rest of it is being ripped out of me and washed straight up the channel towards Portishead. It's an odd sensation; I'm ramping it up and trying to put in a strong finish for the last few hundred metres, but from the beach I doubt it looks as if I'm getting any closer at all. There isn't an easy comparison for this 'finishing straight'. A mountain-top finish in the Tour-de-France may be close, but slowing on the final slopes may translate to taking longer to reach the finish line, but it doesn't mean it actually moves further away. If I slow now I will slip away from the slipway.

My long training swims were worth it just for this moment. After the eight mile one I got out feeling perfectly happy that there were a few miles left in me. A few little twinges, a couple of dull aches, some tangible lethargy, but overall a body which was not yet beaten. Numb of brain with the monotony of it though. I can remember the feeling of the last mile in the lake, and I feel better now than I did then. My confidence that I can put out the necessary watts all the way to the finish is borne of experience, I do not think I am being hoodwinked by adrenaline or the excitement of the moment. Glancing at the boat I catch sight of a yellow swim-cap hovering about at head height among the other figures. Fantastic. Jake is on his way. Close enough for the odd snatch of detail I can increasingly make out a distinct group of figures on the slipway too. This is a real help as the grey concrete of the slipway is hard to pick out against the grey of the stone beach; I have a proper target now. The seaward end of the pier is still to my left, so there must be more than 300 metres to go still, but the strength of the tidal stream ought to be fading with every metre closer to shore and each passing minute. Jake appears beside me, high elbow, classic club-swimmer's stroke. Grins are exchanged, but no embrace or high five. I have to complete the swim without physical contact and he cannot swim ahead of me so as not to break the pace-making rules. Can't really stop for a chat either, gotta keep on top of the tide.

I am level with the pier-head now, Jake is escorting me in and Jo, Stan and Eddie are only about 300 metres away on dry land. Even if I slip a bit off the pace and get dragged by the tide now I will stay this side of the pier and just have an extra few metres to do back along the edge of the beach to hit the official finish point. This is a moment to be savoured, I can mentally relax as long as my arms keep going. I have friends and well-wishers on the boat and on the shore and the gap between them is shortening. Thoughts are rushing in and out of my head with no regard for each other. One second I am ecstatic, then the next brings a panicky feeling and a skipped heartbeat as I quickly check my trunks are still where they should be. A burst of pride as I pause briefly to watch Jake's graceful, easy stroke. Gob-fulls of seawater, the only ones today, as I take too long sighting in the hope of picking out my family from the gathered few. This is not a struggle, but it is the scrappiest bit of swimming I've done all day. No speech prepared for my landing, no idea if I will even be able to stand up. The slipway is a rough old beast to be located and managed by feel alone through the murky water. A gashed shin is a distinctly possible, potentially humbling memento of the final moments. There will be an inevitable, floundering transition from swimming to crawling as I try to reach a point on the slipway surface I am confident enough to use for the attempt to stand up. I do decide to do that while the water is still deep enough to break a fall, but not so deep that a wave could still grab me by the knees and crumble me before the crowd. However it happens, clearing the water unaided and waving to the boat from dry land is the final target, the act which puts the wax seal on my certificate. And that moment, having been too distant to contemplate for most of the morning, is getting closer by the second.

I am near enough to make out the faces. Eddie, Stan and Jo are right at the front, holding a towel and my tracksuit. I was explicitly clear that I wanted to cover myself up as quickly as possible. Warmth being the justification, embarrassment at how I look in a pair of budgie-smugglers being the truth. A respectful few metres behind is a colourful and eclectic pick and mix of friends. There are others dotted about too, strangers on the beach wondering why there is a boat hovering about in the bay and a clutch of passers-by leaning on the railings above the sea wall. They are not here for me and it's not going to be much of a show, but it's satisfying to think that I'm adding something different to their trip to Clevedon sea front. Jake's still here, just to my left and I'm lining up the two edges of the slipway I can see on the beach. Ruby D is much closer than I thought and I can hear Steve shouting to Jake – "Don't let anyone help him out of the water!". He accelerates accordingly, and is right by me, ready to fend off any well-meaning extended hands. My fingers are beginning to brush the surface of the concrete ramp, which signals the end of swimming as I have known it for the past few hours. Both hands are on a firm surface, so I move each one out further to make sure I'm not too close to the invisibly submerged edges. Feels like about knee deep, a couple of cycles of breaststroke, plant my feet and push up. I have only been vertical to tread water and feed, and this is my first contact with a solid surface. Paul sounds Ruby D's horn and there is clapping and cheering, now is not the moment to swoon back down. A few steps through the quickly shallowing water over the slipway, a swagger with a hint of

John Wayne about it, but I'm kept upright by the smiles on my family's faces. Thumbs up and a wave to the boat and my fantastic crew and that is it. Job done.

Soaking in the faces, I am more astounded by the incredible turnout than I am by what I've just done. I feel ok, not particularly tired, and not at all cold. I do very definitely feel exposed though, so grab the towel and my QuickDri tracksuit top and swiftly and clumsily engineer my way into it. Eddie performs well as a leaning post as I hoist the trousers amidships. Unbeknownst to me I am streamed live to the select few, probably garbling some poor attempt at a couple of humorous comments; deflecting my embarrassment at not being mentally prepared to converse with so many genuine well-wishers. Paul and Ruby D perform a miniature victory lap of the bay, a toot of the horn, some waving and cheering and off speed my crew back to Portishead. There is a slight wrench as I feel I should be on the boat with them. But more hands to shake, more pats on the back, more genuinely and flatteringly excited friends, more hugs and squeezes.

Then Jo hands me the best cup of tea I have ever had.

Chapter 6

AFTER THE SWIM

A sense of anti-climax is normal. Previous adventures have all done much the same to me. A couple of hours after the adrenaline recedes my body is busy directing its resources to getting the recovery processes going, leaving little for the brain to work with. I am at home, it is mid-afternoon, and it is a normal day. I swam from Penarth to Clevedon this morning, but now it is a normal day. The TV is on and I'm lying on the bed with a tad of tiredness, a vague semblance of smugness, but a far stronger sense of unease. I feel guilty, somewhat fraudulent. I am certain I made this swim out to be a massive deal, told everyone it was going to be a real test, suggested that I would just need to come home and collapse. But I'm not feeling the exhaustion I expected, and I am now wishing I had planned a more fitting afternoon. I wish I had done the official landing on the slipway then waded back into the water, swum to the boat, made a bit more use of Paul's specially fabricated ladder and spent a few minutes thanking my crew properly. I wish I was sat in a pub now with Jo and my crew, pint in hand, staring out across the sea, enjoying their company and getting the view from the boat. This moment needed the same forethought and planning as everything else, but I neglected it. Has it really all been worth the inconvenience I've put everyone through? Was this just an entirely selfish act? Have I massively over-indulged my sense of self?

Please do not interpret arrogance in this. It was not easy, I had some tough moments, I was tested, but it did not beat me up in the way I genuinely expected it to. Confusion as much as anything else. Clearly my tiredness is contributing to a lack of proportional grasp on my emotions. Congratulations come at me, but the more impressed the congratulator sounds, the less deserved it feels. Pride V Guilt, one on each shoulder, prize bout of the evening.

Keep the tea flowing, that ought to help. Gav has dropped all my kit back from the boat so get some stuff tidied up, recycle the bottles, clean out the big flask, stash the feed-stick and basket in a corner of the garage for…. next time? The afternoon sneaks by and dinner is welcome; despite taking on somewhere near 4000kcal during the swim, I have nonetheless worked up a bit of an appetite. Between little stretching sessions, I fill my evening scrolling through the comments and photographs posted through the day; some from land, some from the boat, some from the other side of the world. Without exception they are positive, joyous, encouraging, excited. Wonderful to read, and they do help with my lull, but I can't bring myself to respond to any of it; I simply can't match the good cheer, can't raise my game. Return a Becker serve with a fishing net instead of a racket? That would be disrespectful and insulting. A congratulatory call from my Mum and Dad makes for a solid boost though.

Over the next few days the positivity begins to seep back in. As people ask about how my swim went it really helps that they stick around for the answer and press for more detail. Thursday, Friday and Saturday mooch by and I can't help but notice the energy of the wind. If I hadn't managed Wednesday, I would have been waiting another two weeks for my next window of opportunity. Hopefully thorough, but struggling to find engagingly different ways to say, 'thank you', I work through all the online comments, the corners of my mouth edging further upwards as I do so.

I get a text from Laura:

"Are you getting the blues going through the photos?"

"Yes, suffered with it a bit yesterday. Really felt like I should respond to all the positivity on the FB group last night. It took hours! Still feeling pretty chuffed about it, but tiredness and blues seem to come in little waves. Some stunning photos though!"

Sunday morning is my opportunity to catch up with Steve at the lake, have a gentle, agenda-less plod up and down, then get my swim recognition form signed off to send to the BLDSA.

Before I change for my swim, I stand on the rocks at the end of the lake, hands in pockets, and stare across to Wales. Other swimmers are gathering; one or two probably know why I'm stood here, most don't, and to some I am an unfamiliar figure. And that's just fine. Last time I was in the marine lake I was just turning my joints over, keeping them fluid during the awkward fortnight of postponement. Not training, just staying topped up. This time, and boy am I looking forward to it, I am rotating those joints to shake out the last of the twinges, squeeze out any remaining stiffness and leave it all in the water. And there, just the other side of the lake wall, that expanse of estuary filling the space between me and the Welsh landscape on the horizon – that's where I had my last swim. The satisfaction of completing something local is simmering away, steaming the thick residue from my airways and lifting my soul on the thermal eddies.

A couple of lengths, thighs and things cosseted in my old familiar jammers. A leisurely transition from near-nude to clothed, punctuated and extended by chit-chat. Catching up with familiar faces, welcoming new ones. Boosted. This is my familiar home ground, but it feels enhanced, filmed in ultra-HD. Characters filled with detail and colour; surround-sound; immersive; smell-o-vision. Bloody hell, it's like real life – but better. The company of swimmers is a mighty, mighty thing.

Over the next few weeks the new school term starts and, as usual, all but obliterates the feeling of living. Recent memories are instantly transported back in time, becoming ancient history. I make it to Clevedon for a sea swim or a few laps of the lake every now and then. If I'm with the kids, I tend to nudge them, point over towards Penarth and say, "See over there......". That's about as far as I get before Jake and Stan roll their eyes and wander off, but Eddie unfailingly answers with, "I'm proud of you, Dad." Must be after something.

We meet for dinner (thanks Steve!) to celebrate the swim and for me to thank my crew. Anticipating a bit of a de-brief I am also slightly nervous about it. This is when I find out how much I irritated the crew. It turns out I didn't smile that much which worried Laura a little – were they doing something wrong? No, I was just busy – I'm pretty certain I said thank you for my feeds though. My most worrying moment, when the crew gathered ominously for what I assumed was a swim-terminating decision, turned out to be Gav showing them the app he was using to document the day in one-second video clips. Steve thought that if I'd fed hourly, and with a bit more purpose, then I may have challenged Gary Carpenter's record and cruised in with the tide from the south rather than battling across it. My feeds were upped for calorific content a bit towards the end as Steve and Laura were concerned I was slowing a bit; I can't fault their judgement on that one - I felt stronger at the end than I did four hours in. When the boat switched sides, I thought it was a navigational thing, but it was more to do with battling the building wind. Overall, it appears we did a good job. They all enjoyed the day out and there is a noticeable enthusiasm to do more exploration of swimming in the Estuary.

An evening gathering of swimmers at the sailing club provides a good moment for Steve to present me with my certificate from the BLDSA. The certificate is significant; I shall (in good time) make a frame for it. Much like I shall (in good time) plot the route on my shipping chart of the Severn Estuary. But as memories go, a firm handshake of approval from Steve, a man of indisputable distance-swimming pedigree, is well and truly up there as a moment of personal significance.

September and October are my favourite time of the year to swim. Spring is exciting; the slow but noticeable rise in sea temperature and associated lengthening of swims, expanding of horizons. But Autumn is better. It is the sea swimmer's secret paradise. All around are layering up, guarding against the chill of the setting sun, sealing out the crisp sea breeze. We strip off and stride in to warm up in the balmy waters, bounce about in the waves as the sun sets beyond the pier. As the rest of the world are closing their curtains, we are warming our backsides on the concrete walkway at the back of the beach. And I am still keen to be here, doing this, no loss of mojo. Two months after my swim and it is slowly finding its place. Yes, I am smug about it (hopefully I don't show it too much). Sunsets over Wales hold something more than just the joy of swathes of colour and although the sea was already a place of comfort for me, I feel at ease, more relaxed, buoyed by it. And this is significant in coming to terms with what I have done. It was never just about getting from A to B, doing it by swimming, start and finish line, tick the box. It was about developing my skills, answering a few personal questions, enhancing my future swimming experience, learning from others, and maybe giving other people something to contemplate. Here I am, a few weeks later, still excited about getting in the water. Looking forward to the icy winter dips, but in no hurry for them to arrive. I have memories of some great swims I did as part of my training, but what I remember most is sharing them with others. The preparation was enjoyable; time consuming, but not onerous; detailed and specific, but worthwhile and far-reaching. I am managing to squeeze a bit of coaching in here and there and quite enjoying the sneaking suspicion that I may actually know what I'm talking about.

Still needling away at me in the background though is the unease, the slightly fraudulent feeling that it wasn't quite tough enough. The more impressed someone is when they ask about it, the more embarrassment I am holding back. I came away uninjured, unstung, I wasn't sick; slight, rubbed-red patches under my arms but no loss of skin. A small graze on my left shoulder from chin-scuffing and the obligatory goggle-induced red rings around the eyes – that's as close as I got to battle scars. Apart from during my over-excited sighting of the slipway during the last few hundred yards, I swallowed no seawater – despite plenty of white-caps and face slaps. My hat stayed on, my goggles and earplugs didn't leak. Cramp was a no-show, my two-piece collarbone kept quiet. I hung on to my strength well enough to get somewhere near our anticipated route, no headaches, no migraine, no swelling of lips, tongue or throat. If the swim wasn't tough enough to throw any of this at me, then maybe it wasn't much of a challenge at all. I am also very aware that I cannot swim 15.3 miles in six hours, and I know the tide well enough to understand just how much of the work it did. Yes, I had to fight it in the last stretch, but that was just a consequence of allowing it to rush me on earlier in the swim. I find it awkward when asked about the distance. I lead with, "Just under 13 miles in a straight line". They counter, "But the boat tracker says you actually did over 15 miles, wow!". And I parry, "In reality though, in number of strokes and energy terms, I probably only swam about 11 miles".

An assembly presentation beckons, not to the whole school, just to the year 10 and 11 students in the house my tutor group are part of. My attempt at a message is threefold; humanising teachers (we do stuff too, you know), encouraging a positive view of challenge, and empathy with what we expect of them (I reckon this swim is about the equivalent of a GCSE or A level). "A Journey by Numbers" – twenty photographs, each with a number for me to expand on. A plate piled high with food, the number 500, extra daily calories I took on in the few weeks prior to the swim. A picture of a wave, with Flat Holm in the background (Laura assures me I am in the shot, but behind the wave), the number 1, height in metres of many of those waves we encountered in the central section. A screenshot of the track of a training swim during which friends swam or kayaked alongside me, the number 30, an estimate of how many people offered their time and expertise to help me. You get the idea.

I doubt that any of the students took as much away from the assembly as I did though. This was the beginning of banishing my unease, flushing out my fear of being a phony. Stacking up the numbers, doing the sums, linking the variables. Over ten thousand strokes with each arm and no shoulder issues – that was in no small part because during the three months before the swim, I accumulated about ninety minutes in each of the strengthening or stretching positions Laura had given me. In the last few years I have focussed on my stroke, paid careful attention to the different ways in which I can recover my arm, learnt to vary my technique, share out the stress and strain and give my muscles the chance to switch on and off, recovering during the stroke. Sickness didn't trouble me despite the sloshing of liquid feeds in lumpy seas; that was because I tested and re-tested my feed regime in the lake, adapting it after the growling stomach from the first test. Accurately measured, the record of my speed variation with time gave Steve and Paul something tangible to work with as they adapted the route to the conditions. My feeds arrived promptly and with the right stuff in the basket; Gav and Laura were perfectly capable of mixing my feeds as we went, but there was no need to as the schedule was set, the bottles were prepared, and I'd spent time coding them with coloured cable-ties. This all brings me back to the approach I felt I had to adopt. Do everything I possibly could to mitigate threats, to reduce the impact of 'bad luck' and increase the likelihood of 'good luck'.

At last, months after the success of the day, an appreciation of where that success came from is beginning to sink in, where and when my responses to the challenge were implemented; how and why potentially adverse conditions just became enjoyable variations. Every little question I asked, every moment browsing through other people's experiences of feed methods. Every time I concentrated on my stroke, used my Focus Points, "Melons on the Wall", "Paparazzi", "Bish-Bosh-Whooooosh", "Floppy Water-Balloon" and "Cracking Walnuts" (to name a few). Every time I caught myself stood in an assembly, part listening, but mostly paying attention to my shoulder-blade position as I raised my arms to the side and practised isolating the movement of my forearm from my shoulder. Every swim, every wave, every variation of pace as I swam with others - sometimes chasing, sometimes pacing. Every. Single. Thing.

I could have made it more heroic, a bigger battle, left myself some obstacles to overcome on the day. I could have done the research, but not the testing; trained for the distance, but not for the conditions; trained, but not prepared. Perhaps I would have crawled onto the slipway, shoulders wrenched and ruined by the waves, taste of vomit and brine still strong in my mouth, but feeling like a real hero – battle-scars to prove it.

Which is where the writing comes in. There have been a few nags, polite enquiries, "When are you going to do a little article?", "Have you done a blog?", but I hadn't really felt it was worth space on a page until now, at the point of nearly finishing. With each paragraph I am retiring doubts, resolving the unease, gaining a greater appreciation of what we did, how fortunate I have been, the enormity of what others have done for me. I am back to the major and minor influences, how they layer up, interlock and coalesce. I did the preparation. I did the swim. Those facts remain even if I do not write. Thousands of words later I have a deeper understanding of their relative significance. These hours of prodding the keyboard have all helped me to reduce the amplitude of my wavering, and I edge closer to the asymptote of satisfaction in a job well done. As I re-read it feels horribly self-indulgent, perhaps just a cathartic exorcising of personal demons, but maybe, just maybe, of value for others to read? Just like the swim itself, which to some may seem like an insurmountable obstacle, but to others just a few hours training, this wodge of words may hold fascination for one reader where another finds turgid monotony. That's not for me to decide or concern myself with.

But now I know my swim.

Chapter 7

WHAT NEXT?

"What's next?". "When are you going to swim the (English) Channel?". Laura's asked me the second one as many times as everybody else put together.

There are so many reasons why the English Channel is not on my radar at the moment, some of those have been hinted at. That's not a discussion for here. My swim took two minutes less than six hours. Two minutes too short to count as a qualifying swim for the English Channel. This is a great illustration of how hard it is to draw lines and set standards for such a difficult and variable environment as the open water. If I had been a slower swimmer, would I therefore be better qualified for a bigger swim because I was in the water for longer? Am I less qualified than someone who took longer, but crawled out of the water battered, bruised and dizzy? No matter, I am not trying to qualify for anything other than my own next step.

A bigger swim would be an obvious natural progression, but it can't just be about the size of the swim. I feel I could do bigger, but I wouldn't want to add miles just for the sake of miles. I am keen to avoid the "next rung of the ladder" effect. All of us are stood part-way up the ladder, with a fog allowing us to see just a few rungs ahead. Aspirational, of course, to see what those just above us are doing. Natural to do what is necessary to take that step up yourself. But is it inevitable that this process should continue endlessly? The Swanage to Studland swim that I described earlier moved me a rung up the ladder and got me thinking about bigger things. With each step up, the view ahead shifts up too and the Bristol Channel rung came into focus through the fog. Now I have made it onto that rung I am more aware of the stages further ahead; the other channels, the oceans seven swimmers, the ultra-marathons in lakes as long as counties. That's not for me right now. I would like to take this opportunity to look sideways, admire the view to the horizon from the height I've already achieved. If I could afford the English Channel, I would rather spend it going to Australia to visit my relatives there and maybe have a crack at Rottnest instead. There is more to do in my fascinating local waters. Penarth and back maybe, but less as a distance challenge and more as an exercise in logistics – experimenting with different routes. I quite fancy trying to see if it's possible to leave Clevedon Beach at high water, swim with the outgoing tide past Flat Holm, turn to the south-east for a mile or two then slingshot round Steep Holm as the tide turns and ride the flow back to Clevedon. That would need some serious thought and would be at least double the swim I've just done. But I'm not sure I'm that bothered by doing it all myself, I would just like to see if it's possible. Perhaps I would swim the outward journey, hop back on the boat and Laura or Steve might like to leap in and swim back? No rules to worry about, no official observers to satisfy. If a distance crossing starts to attract me, then why not stay in these waters, but just head a bit further west? North Devon to South Wales has only been done a few times and as yet does not have a franchised feel to it (though I fear it won't be long). But for now, I just intend to look around, enjoy the view, avoid the inevitable neck-cramp of constantly squinting up the ladder into the fog.

So I may take on another swim-based adventure, but not just yet. The disruption and training time wouldn't be fair on my family two years in a row, and I have other things to think about for the time being. Swimming isn't going anywhere, neither is the water.

A better challenge for me right now would be to continue developing my coaching, help others to have a go, extend their horizons. What have I done so far that I've enjoyed and has felt more like giving than taking?

- Encouraged winter dippers and helped nervous swimmers to be more comfortable in the open water.

- Helped triathletes deal positively with the ugly realisation that swimming is the toughest of the three disciplines (but doesn't have to be): Laura and I are already running sessions together aimed at all this and more.

- Taken a close group of friends on the afore-mentioned trip from Swanage to Knoll Beach.

- With my friend Charlie, jointly organised swim trips to Old Harry Rock in Studland and encouraged a large group of swim-pals from Lulworth to Durdle Door and back; this we are likely to do again, but perhaps it's time we at least covered our costs?

- Through a sport and mental health initiative, taken two local teenagers through a course of six sessions learning about how to cope with the open water, how to risk assess swim spots and conditions, how to plan a swim expedition; they have since sent me photographs of their swims in the Lake District and Slovenia.

- Helped novice swimmers to hone their cold-water sprint technique, shaving off smidgens of seconds here and there, and make it into the top ten in the world at the Cold Water Swimming Championships in Estonia.

This is all so different from the restrictive curriculum I am compelled to deliver in the overly (but necessarily) structured school environment. All sorts of people want to get in the water for all sorts of reasons – it is an area where money-crunching franchises or restricted and clearly defined pathways are not always appropriate. It is very definitely not a place for "one size fits all" or for big, visible logos. This is all about individuality, personal goals, "this works for me, thanks", whatever gets you in the water. How else can I help? And what better place to do it than in the Bristol Channel, at Clevedon Marine Lake, within my local community where a vast range of experience, at all levels, can be drawn on?

Of course, I still fully intend to keep getting in the water, wherever I can. Trunks and towel always in the back of the van. The sea pulls strongest. My local pool serves its purpose, but its abundant chemicals do not cleanse my soul. Solitary time in the water is an important part of my swimosphere, but I am also blessed with a diverse set of friends to frolic about with, all of whom have different, favourite ways and places to swim. Company of swimmers – that's a given. Jaunts off Clevedon Beach are group gatherings by necessity, the tide makes it that way; we have swimmers heading off a mile up the coast, some happy just to walk in up to their waist, and everything in between. Some are there just to hold a brolly for their loved ones to change under and give them a warming hug, but they are still a part of the swimming fold. We all still try to leave time for a chat, hear about each other's swims. I have yet to regret a swim, though I often head home feeling bad that I didn't have time to catch up with everyone: but there will always be next time.

Chapter 8

FANCY IT YOURSELF?

I f you are in any way tempted to have a go at this swim, then I would suggest at least four things you should do, over and above the standard endurance training you might otherwise embark on for a marathon sea swim. Of course, when I got over my Cornish-born, blue-water-snobbery and decided swimming in the brown stuff here may not be all that bad, I didn't know that this swim was in my sights. I have been tweaking and tending to my stroke development and learning about the estuary since long before swimming across it ever became a realistic proposition: observing and discussing its idiosyncrasies, responding to its temperament and habituating myself to its customs and rituals. But if I could simmer down the sauce of my accumulated knowledge to a rich gravy for savouring in a concentrated form, then drizzling it across the following four courses might just create a big enough dinner to sate your need for knowledge. Consider these the absolute minimum study requirements.

- Swim in Clevedon Marine Lake.

- Spend a day in Clevedon, observing the channel, and include a research swim in the bay by the pier.

- Join in with a swim from the pier to Ladye Bay and back, in relatively challenging conditions.

- Organise and execute a swim from Battery Point (Portishead) to Clevedon Beach.

Swim in Clevedon Marine Lake

Ideally, just after it has been refreshed and stirred up by an overtopping tide. This water is silty. When you swim you will not be able to see your arms beneath you, a burst of bubbles is the best you can hope to spot. When you breathe the world momentarily returns, but with elusive detail obscured by the splish and splosh of your stroke and the chop of the day. This is not what most people are used to, and you need to know if and how it affects you. You may notice it is not quite as salty as most coastal seas, though still salty enough to get to your mouth and throat which will affect you over a long swim. There is added buoyancy over swimming pools, lakes, rivers and hot-tubs, but not quite as much as further out in the clear blue seas found around most other parts of our coast. The bottom of the lake is silty mud and rocks; the same as to be found along the edges of the estuary at any likely entry and exit points for a crossing. Be mindful of possible debris finding its way onto the bottom of the lake, but get some contact with your hands and feet to prepare you for the potential scrabble in and out of the estuary. Practise your sighting, notice how other users appear from nowhere in your on/off blindness. Like a huge infinity pool, the lake affords you a view of the estuary: fixate on the pier and break off to look across to Wales. Far enough away for a challenge, but close enough to be tantalisingly possible? Lake aperitif whetted your appetite? Then indulge in the three-course taster dinner described below. Should that fill and thrill you, then consider gorging on the full banquet.

Spend a day in Clevedon

Make sure you are here long enough to see the tide go through a full cycle. Preferably on a spring tide. If you can, watch it race in across the mudflats and sandbanks. Maybe hop a junction down the M5 and walk out to the tip of Sand Point, preferably at low water. Stare out past Steep Holm and Flat Holm, then across to Wales. Look north-east to Clevedon and its pier, across the top of the sandbanks. On a clear day, you can see the entire swim from Penarth to Clevedon and, if the tide is low enough, you can observe some of the terrain too. Go back to Clevedon and have a swim in the sea, by the pier at high water. Stay in for at least an hour, with high water slap-bang in the middle of your dip, hovering in and around the bay and the pier. Tread water under the pier a few times during the hour to experience the speed of the flow, and how quickly it changes direction from incoming to outgoing. No slack water here. Maybe 15 minutes after high water, go out to about half way along the pier, position yourself under one of the arches and point yourself into the outgoing tide, straight up the coast; swim against the tide, perpendicular to the pier, as if doing a 25m sprint and see how far from the pier you get. Let the flow drift you back under the pier arch and repeat the short sprint. Do this until you can no longer make progress against the flow and note the time. How long is it after the turn of the tide? Now get yourself back to the beach, hobble over the pebbles and get togged up. Crack open your flask, arm yourself with some cake to offer about and have a good chat with the other swimmers on the beach. Considerable swimming history splashes, sits and strolls around this beach on a daily basis. Some are dippers but have done it almost every day for decades. Some are serious about distance swimming, either because they still do it, or because they've done it in the distant past, in the days before every stroke and sentiment was blogged and logged, photographed and flounced. Many have done big swims of their own, plenty are preparing for their own challenges and a good number have supported others. You may find some who have crewed for English or North Channel swims, you may have a chat with someone who organises swim-runs and aquathlons, perhaps you'll shake hands with an ice-miler or two. There will certainly be plenty willing to share their experience and offer some advice about this stretch of water. With any luck, you'll pick up a few golden nuggets to help you plan the next two things you should do.

Swim to Ladye Bay and back

Do not do this on your own, join in with a group who are planning to swim from the pier to Ladye Bay and back. When the times of the tides allow, many weekend days in the warmer seasons you will find a group gathering on the beach for such a venture; meeting time will be around 45 minutes before high water. Ideally, do it on a day with a surge of swell and a bit of chop, and hopefully a noticeable, prevailing south-westerly wind of up towards 10 mph. Be absolutely sure that they are conditions you can cope with for more than an hour, but if it's too calm then it will be a much-reduced educational opportunity. The sea in the bay is often a tad calmer than you will encounter slightly further up the coast. Once you head off under the pier, with the tide, there is little chance of an exit until you get to Ladye Bay and you cannot turn around and go back until the tide grants you permission. I can't be sure, as conditions are never quite the same, but you ought to get a pretty good taste of how changeable the swimming experience can be though the immediate appearance of the sea may not change much during the hour. Notice how the regulars time their launch from the beach almost to the minute; even a small gathering of single numbers may still head off as two separate groups, a few minutes apart. They know their tide times and they know their speed. Ideally, you will have made the effort to have met some of them on a previous occasion at the beach for a swim. If not, then expect to be grilled (in a friendly way) on your speed and competence in these conditions, while they decide if they are willing to take the responsibility of swimming with you and advise on who you would be best to swim with.

On your way up towards Ladye Bay, do some of your swim close to the rocks and some further out. Notice the difference in the waves, swell and frequency of breakers. It's not hard to figure out that the swell and motion of the waves is less predictable closer to land and there is more white water. Reflected swell from the rocks and sharply shallowing water causes the energy in the waves to hap-hazardly bounce about, jockeying you how it sees fit. It is easier to swim further out. But log this disturbance effect in your databank because similar changes of conditions over just a few metres also exist way out in the channel itself as you pass from shallow to deep to shallow again, or into the shadow of nearby islands or rocks beneath you. Monitor your progress along the coast by taking a good look at the buildings high above the rocks – try not to fixate on a particular one as you will likely begin to swim in an arc around it, it is better to watch the gaps between them as they open up and close again. Can you detect the difference in your speed as the tidal flow begins to ease? If you have the prevailing wind coming up the channel from the south-west in the same direction as the tidal flow, then you are swimming wind with tide. The waves come from behind you, or over your left shoulder. The forward slope of each wave is relatively gentle, and you rise and fall to a consistent rhythm, sometimes even feeling as if you are gently surfing the down slopes and gaining some advantage from the elliptical flow of energy in each wave. Remember, enjoy, savour this feeling. Approaching Ladye Bay you will have a vastly different experience depending on where you are. The bay is tucked in to the south of a small, rocky headland which interacts with the flow differently depending on direction and speed. Should you arrive a bit before the turn and there is still a little pace in the incoming tide then there will probably be a clockwise eddy in the bay. Approaching the bay close to the rocky shore, you will encounter resistance, and probably convince yourself the tide has already turned. It is faster to stay out and aim for the tip of the rocky headland, turning in just a few metres before it to be carried in to the beach by the clockwise flow. Crawling in the shallows on an unseen, unstable, rolling rock surface, unsteadily rising to a stagger up onto the pebbled beach, it is likely that you will feel you are half-way through your swim.

In purely distance terms, you are at the mid-point. But if energy, effort and time are your measures, you are only about one third of the way through. The tide will hopefully be about to turn and it may seem reasonable to imagine that ahead of you is simply a mirrored version of what you have just completed. Did you use the high tide time for Clevedon? If so then it will be about 5 minutes later here at Ladye Bay, just 1400m further up the coast. Ten minutes beyond the high water time at Clevedon and it is fairly certain the flow has reversed and will soon pick up pace, any earlier than that and the first few hundred yards of your return journey may well be hard-going and slow. An anti-clockwise eddy within the bay swirls into life which will make leaving by following the rocks appear as if the tide has not turned at all (exactly the opposite of the sense of it on approach). Head out at 45 degrees to the coastline for fifty metres or so then turn to set your sights on the pier. Remember the feeling of the waves on the outward journey? Don't expect the same on the way back. We are now in wind against tide territory and you will be swimming with the tide, but against the wind and waves as they approach from about 45 degrees to your right. If conditions were not as I described earlier, perhaps calmer with just a foot of swell or chop and gentle winds, then the flowing tide may sap the energy out of it and flatten the surface. Hopefully though, you have 3 feet or more of surface variation and winds up near the 10mph mark. It is possible that the waves look a little lower than on the way out – the tidal flow perhaps now leeching a little energy out from under the waves and dropping them in height. Yes, you now have the tide with you and if you can float, you will make it back to the pier. But with proper waves trundling towards you, the tidal flow now makes each one a more intimidating beast. The oncoming, forward slope (now an upslope for you) will be steeper than before. The energy of the wave is rotating more quickly, so the top overtakes the water below it creating turbulence, white water and possibly breakers. Think of the energy within a wave as a rolling barrel carrying the wave forwards, then imagine the tidal flow beneath it as a travellator. We have a series of barrels (waves) rolling along the travellator. On the way to Ladye Bay, the travellator and the barrels were rolling in the same direction as you were trying to travel, and your job was to slide your way along the top of the barrels, everything working together. But now we are on the way back. The barrels are still trying to make their way towards Ladye Bay, but the travellator has switched direction beneath them, so they have to spin much more rapidly. To make progress, you are now trying to pull yourself along the top of the barrels against the direction of their now faster rotation. Surfers making their way out from a beach often 'duck-dive' the oncoming waves: in this analogy they are squeezing themselves between the barrels and the travellator and being squirted out the back of the wave like heavy cotton undies through a mangle.

Realistically, as a swimmer, duck-diving is not an efficient choice once we are out in the normal swell. We employ a surface stroke where the rhythm, breathing and relaxed recovery of our arms above the water is all part of making a long-distance swim possible. If the waves are big enough to make duck-diving worthwhile, we probably shouldn't be out for a distance swim anyway. We have to deal with the shape and nature of the waves as we meet them. In these conditions they slap you in the face when you mistime your breathing or sighting, the oncoming, steep slope diverts your forward momentum upwards, but then leaves you with less water to get a propelling hand into on the other side. The very nature of white water is that it has lost its density, so it is harder to gain a good catch and it does not reward you with resistance during the pull. Perhaps a deeper, straight-arm stroke may help, but have you trained for this? Can your shoulders cope? This is the same day, the same weather, the same swimmer, but a very different swim from your outward journey. But don't worry, you will make it back as long as you can stay afloat. The tide will carry you towards the pier and although the waves feel as if they are pushing you backwards, they are really just pitching you up and down and reducing the effectiveness of your stroke.

As you progress back towards Clevedon Beach you have the option of going around the end of the pier, but ideally only do it if you have plenty left in the tank and you're with someone else of similar strength who knows what to expect. Stop swimming momentarily as you pass the end of the pier to observe how quickly the tide carries you. Once around the end turn quickly for the beach, but beware of fishermen's lines. They will come a long way out from the pier as they fish the outgoing tide. Try to swim on a path parallel to the pier and note the direction you have to aim to achieve this. If you were in a kayak right now, you would be ferrygliding: pointing yourself into the current, but slightly angled towards the beach to your right. The flow would rush down the left edge of your kayak and push you sideways towards the beach. All you would have to do is maintain a 'forward' speed to stop the current also dragging you backwards. Unfortunately, although the principle is the same for a swimmer, the physics is far less generous. We are not as streamlined or efficient as a kayak, slicing through the water cleanly, nor do we have a long, smooth flank for the water to push against. Nonetheless, you will need to aim back towards Ladye Bay, but with your body angled to the right to take you towards the landing point on the beach. This is tiring work for apparently little reward, but if you have the energy, you should be able to maintain a fixed distance from the pier whilst edging closer to the beach. Don't panic if you begin to tire and the current starts to push you backwards. If you reach this state then a new approach is needed in which you no longer waste energy fighting the tide. Just accept that you need to aim yourself perpendicular to the shore and swim directly across the flow towards land. Do not fixate on your intended landing point on the beach as this will turn you back into the tide again. Stay with the cross-flow body position and you will make it back to land but a bit further down the coast. You may just have to clamber over some rocks and walk a minute or two back to where you left your kit. If you don't fancy the rocks, then stick close to them and allow the tide to take you a bit further round to the next beach. Longer walk in your cossie, but less chance of rock-clambering injuries.

I am not suggesting this always presents itself as a tough swim, but there is plenty to observe and learn in just a small stretch of the channel. Subtle changes in wind speed or direction, the difference between spring and neap tides, ambient air pressure or a degree or two of variance in sea temperature. Combined with the fast and rapidly changing tide, these factors create a mixed bag of swim conditions. No two swims are the same. Wrench the lid off your cake tin once more and get your inquisitive ears on. Chat away. Discuss today's swim and how it compares with the best and worst the swimmers have seen.

There are strong, confident swimmers here who frequently sail up and down this bit of coast as if knocking out a mile in the pool, but likely still have a tale of the time it caught them out, turned their legs to jelly, put them over its knee and showed them who was boss. Respect for this bit of the estuary is rightly strong here. No matter how experienced, the locals will think things through every time they get in. Plans will be shared; conditions will be observed, analysed and discussed; forecasts checked and cross-checked; timings proposed, verified and agreed. An agenda, conference table and flip-chart may not be apparent, but during the affable pre-swim chit-chat you can rest assured that this process is taking place.

Head home from this swim and allow time to ponder it all. If you plan to do it again then when the time comes, gather what information you can and try to envisage the conditions you will encounter on arrival at the beach. Assuming you remain attracted to the idea of crossing the channel then apply what happens here, close to the coast, to what may happen a few miles out. The speed of the tide, the proximity of the estuary bed and the sharp changes in depth. Moving in and out of the shelter of, and turbulence created by headlands and islands will give waves and currents new character and subtle variations in challenge. What would you do to prepare yourself for this potentially abundant variety? Some of it can be mitigated or avoided by choices made on land; when to swim, what route to attempt, the scope of weather conditions you are willing to embrace. Others you just have to accept as a possibility and be ready to deal with on the day.

Swim from Portishead to Clevedon

Notice I suggested you plan it yourself. Any opportunity for a decent length training swim should be embraced, especially in the estuary itself, and there are chances to learn in the water just as with the Ladye Bay swim, but this exercise is really about appreciating and accepting the hierarchy. The tide is King, uncompromising ruler of all, influence and spies in every tiniest outpost of the realm you wish to cross. The wind, sun, cloud, rain, high and low pressures are the gentry, the Lords of the land, each with their claim to the realm: they will tax and tithe you as you pass through their fields, cross their borders. Your family; your job; your daily, monthly, weekly routine; they are Mayor of the town, factory boss, farm-owner, foreman. They offer you work, home comforts, food; you can't do this without their currency, their love, their support, but they only dish it out on their terms: they are boss of you, when you sleep, when you eat, when you move. Who then, are you? You are the serf, the peasant, in your sweat-soaked, rough, hessian tunic, lying in the mud with dreams of freedom and riches on the other side of the channel. You must work the system, negotiate and bob-a-job; pimp yourself out wherever and whenever you can, all the while stuffing the loose, forgotten pennies of energy and knowledge into your satchel. Building up the brownie-points and amassing good will wherever you can. Stealing away in the night or early hours of the morning to practise your bush-craft, honing your skills, steeling your resistance for the journey ahead. You must plan, steal a map, plot your course and time your escape to best avoid the rulers of the land you wish to pass through; seek out compatriots, partners in crime who will hide you when needed and guide you over the mountain passes.

Start by listing the days you have available, then work with the tide times to identify which of those can actually be done. What are the parameters? Choice is limited here as you can only enter the water to start your swim at Portishead at, or shortly after, high water. How early are you willing to start, and how long do you think the swim will take you? It would be smart to make sure your expected arrival time at Clevedon is well before the onset of darkness. Swimming with the tide will be faster than you are used to and get quicker as the swim goes on. Have a really good look at the map, where can you get out if the swim needs to be abandoned? You will be spotted from the coast path or cliff-top properties and it will be an unusual sight for many people, so don't be surprised if someone calls the coastguard. Really, you should let them know you are intending to do the swim and confirm details for them just before you set off. Unless the conditions are clearly difficult, they will be supportive, but don't be surprised if they quiz you a bit. How many of you swimming? Do you have a craft supporting you? Do you have food and drink? Do you have a means of calling for help? Have you checked your phone for signal in this area? Who is your land support, and can they have their name and number please? Please let them know when you are out of the water.

What questions should you be asking yourself? How confident are you in the stability of the weather conditions and forecast for the next three hours? Are you completely sure that you will make the swim? Who are you doing it with? Have they done it before? How well do you know their swim-personality? What happens to them when they get tired or scared? This is not a "try it and see" situation in which you can shorten your route or turn back if you start to struggle or the conditions worsen. One positive is that the tide will take you to Clevedon, if you can stay afloat, but you will need to keep warm and have some strength to guide yourself in to the beach. Fortunately, your end point is easily visible from a mile away, so as the pier approaches you have the chance to begin your exit strategy. Being a couple of hours after the tide has turned, you will be unlikely to be able to get around the end of the pier and back in to the beach, so start to come in close and aim for one of the pier arches nearest the shore. Is this a spring or a neap tide? So will you be able to exit on the beach, or will you have to head for the slipway? Have you practised that? Don't forget you are finishing a few miles from where you started, so have you got all your stuff where you need it? And what has the weather been like, was the wind kind to you, or was it the prevailing south-westerly chop-slapping you in the face with every breath? If it wasn't easy, why not, and what could you do to make it easier next time? If it was easy, was that luck or planning? Were the conditions kind to you, and if so, should you do it again sometime to seek out a little more testing adversity? Learn, learn, learn.

All four of these tasks tucked under your belt and you should know by now if you are serious about swimming the Bristol Channel. An action plan should be forming, your training commitment will be manifesting a sense of scale and a long checklist of the necessary skill-set should begin to gather ticks.

Of course, you don't have to put yourself through this familiarisation process, you could take the blinkered approach and try to find a pilot and a coach/organiser who know the score, understand the local conditions and can plan it all for you. Unlike the English Channel though, nobody here makes a living out of doing this. Only six or seven days in each month have suitable tides for the swim, so it can only be a hobby or a side-line for someone with a boat. The skipper may know the channel, but do they know swimming? If you can find an available, willing and qualified team then pay them suitably and they will sort out the dates and times, tell you when and where to be ready, what to bring with you and then hopefully steer you across. But you've just reduced the scope and interest of the challenge to a largely physical one. Aside from a couple of swims in this murky water just to get yourself used to it then you would probably get away with doing your training in pretty much any open water environment. However, all decisions will lie with your pilot and crew, and if you don't understand the channel, you may not understand their decisions. If they don't know, for sure, what you are capable of, they will have to make decisions very much on the conservative side; it's possible that you will be pulled out of the water, even though you are feeling strong, if it becomes apparent you won't make it across. Without an understanding of the channel, without being closely involved in the planning, without having worked and swum with one of the crew, you may not understand and may be extremely frustrated by the decision. To increase your chances of success your crew have to know, and have trust in, what you can deliver on the day. If you have told them you swim at 2mph, they will have planned a route based on that. If it turns out that this is your speed for the first hour, but it drops off significantly and unpredictably after that, then it may not be possible to confidently re-adjust once underway. Perhaps it could be adapted, but although you may only have slowed by 10%, the alternative may require you to be in the water for 30% longer as you have to give in to the tide until it weakens enough for you to break free of it. The crew can't adopt this plan unless they have absolute faith that the extra 30% is within your capabilities. This is not a "book a slot and follow the rules" swim. If you really embrace the full challenge of this, then you are committing to an apprenticeship, you are learning about yourself. Make sure you know your stuff, because the water will test you on it.

Afterword

There was likely a time, not so many years ago, when I would have taken a stroll along the sea front and gazed out over the water. In front of me would have been a small child, one of my sons. He is all wrapped up, blanket over his legs, woolly hat and mittens somewhere near where they are supposed to be. He'd have been cosy as I pushed him along in some sort of wheeled device, backside warmed by wee-soaked underwear; the raw sea breeze dragging a mixture of dribble and snot across his cheek to its crusty destination in the wrinkles of his neck. I would have steered him up to the railings along the sea wall to look out at the waves. Being a crisp, sunny day, I expect we had to shuffle in alongside another family. Too young and confused to respect social convention, at the sight of the sea he would have excitedly thrown his hat over the wall, uncontrollably wiggled his legs, inadvertently kicked a nearby toddler in the ribs then enthusiastically and loudly garbled some incomprehensible monologue to anyone who'd listen. Hopefully, my apology to the toddler and her mum would have been accepted gracefully and I most likely attempted to lighten the situation by explaining that my child was probably just trying to tell them how much he'd like to get in there for a swim. As I wheeled him away again, dodging the disbelieving gaze of the toddler's mum, I expect I patted him on his now uncovered, bald head and proudly reassured him, "One day son, you will. You will, and I'll be there to watch you."

There will likely come a time, not so many years from now, when I will be taken for a stroll along the sea front to gaze out over the water. Behind me will be a middle-aged man, one of my sons. I am all wrapped up, blanket over my legs, woolly hat and mittens somewhere near where they are supposed to be. I will be cosy as he pushes me along in some sort of wheeled device, backside warmed by wee-soaked underwear; the raw sea breeze dragging a mixture of dribble and snot across my cheek to its crusty destination in the wrinkles of my neck. He will steer me up to the railings along the sea wall to look out at the waves. Being a crisp, sunny day, I expect we will have to shuffle in alongside another family. Too old and confused to respect social convention, at the sight of the sea I will excitedly throw my hat over the wall, uncontrollably wiggle my legs, inadvertently kicking a nearby toddler in the ribs then enthusiastically and loudly garble some incomprehensible monologue to anyone who'll listen. Hopefully, my son's apology to the toddler and her mum will be accepted gracefully and he will most likely attempt to lighten the situation by explaining that I am probably just trying to tell them that I swam across that channel when I was a younger man. As he wheels me away again, dodging the disbelieving gaze of the toddler's mum, I expect he'll pat me on my now uncovered, bald head and proudly reassure me, "One day dad, you did. You did, and I was there to watch you."

Acknowledgements

I set out to write a short article about my swim much as would be of interest to the readership of a magazine – plenty had been keen for me to do so. At two thousand words I had barely set the scene. It continued to grow. I decided to let it expand and resolved to sculpt it back down to a svelte form once my thoughts and recollections had fizzled out. And still it grew. I asked a trusted friend to look it over, expecting by return the reality check, putting me back in my place; the crass, pointless and intolerable scratched from the manuscript and just the essentials left, interesting enough in their own right that even I couldn't dull them down. But back came the encouragement to continue, adorned with constructive and positive suggestions for expansion, a desire to hear more. So in equal measure I apportion blame and express my gratitude to Emma Pusill. An active champion of the wet and cold, and very much a part of the local expertise and enthusiasm I have been fortunate to draw upon over the past few years. Thank you!

I would have had nothing to write about though, if it were not for those who have sown the seeds of ideas, encouraged me and helped me get to the completion of the swim.

I thank the triumvirate of James Bevis, Rachael Davis and Jeremy Murgatroyd – disconnectedly, yet strangely coordinated – for getting me out of the pool and into the big brown. James – a few simple nags and links to bargain wetsuits. Rach – badgering me to partner her for the Dart 10K. Jeremy – introducing me to the rituals, regulations and residents of Clevedon Beach.

Gavin Price for his significant part in quietly and effectively (with all sorts of assistance and enthusiasm from many, many others) growing a community around the Marine Lake and Clevedon Beach. What an incredible sea of knowledge and experience we have to immerse ourselves in.

Marlens, the charity which maintains Clevedon Marine Lake and secured sufficient lottery funding for it to be refurbished: keeping it available and free to use for the local (and widening) community. A dedicated and selfless bunch. Their ethos of availability and participation is as important to me as the water in the lake itself. I have grown loyal to the lake, I encourage others to use it and I want to share it in a way I never could for a paid, business-run venue.

After one swim together and a gentle quizzing over a coffee, Steve Cox asked me a question which I have thus far answered 'no' – but I am grateful for him asking (many times) as it was the seed of this swim. "Do you fancy the (English) Channel then?". More importantly, following a serene Portishead to Clevedon swim with Jo McCready-Fallon, Steve and I began to wonder if we should be encouraging each other to have a crack at the Bristol Channel. Thank you, Steve and Jo.

Susie Baker and all her South West Seals disciples for getting me through a winter of dunking my doughnuts regardless of temperature, priming me for an early start to my outdoor distance training season, and for having a barrel-load of collective enthusiasm to feed from.

In a less specific, but far more significant way, thank you to my family: Jo, Jake, Stan and Eddie for tolerating and encouraging me sneaking off to get some wet hours in at often inconvenient times. Their patience in listening to me go round in circles over every decision in the build up to the swim is hugely appreciated. It is also important that I apologise, publicly, for the stress and worry I have caused, for Jo in particular, from

150

the moment I first announced I intended to do the swim through to my first steps up the slipway, clearly having survived.

Thank you to my Beach Reception Gang: (Really sorry if I've forgotten anyone!)

Jo, Stan, and Eddie; front row with towels and tea.

Suneil Basu, Chris Budd, Steve Lines, Deb Peters, Lynette Blanchard, Pete Gillespie (and kids), Clare Mactaggart, Vicky Bellamy, Richard Nuell, Gavin Price, Rachael and Tony Davis; and a little later on, Nancy Farmer.

And an apology to Debbie Usoro, Helen Slater and a few others who were headed for the beach but missed me because I was too early.

More than thanks to my Crew. The swim simply could not have happened without them.

Paul Wells, Steve Price, Laura Nesbitt, Gavin Oliver and Jake Richardson.

Appendices

Appendix A - THE BOAT CREW

Steve Price – By virtue of vast experience, the ringmaster of this particular circus. English Channel, North Channel, Bristol Channel (there and back in a day). He's been through the failures and successes of far bigger swims than mine. His fondness and fascination for this stretch of water bursts out of him with the slightest of prods and from the moment he realised I was serious about swimming it his presence on the boat had been a constant. If he was a rock, he'd be granite; an egg, sunny side up; an actor, Tom Hanks blended with Brian Blessed. Though he and I had not swum together it was clear that he knew what and who to ask to quickly make up his mind if I was worth the investment of time.

Jo McCready-Fallon – A scholar, a strategist and a Bristol Channel crosser too. We have shared a couple of significant swims, talked a good game and consequently discovered we also share a similar relationship with the open water. Jo was the consultant I needed to help me find my own route through the preparation. We don't always want our questions answered with another, but Jo knows when that is necessary and exactly how big the question mark should be. Sadly, Jo couldn't join me on the boat on the final date of the swim, though I'm pleased to say it was because he had planned a sizeable swim of his own on the Dorset coast. Seventy miles apart, but sharing the same south-easterly and, bless him, I think he tamed it a little for me on its way past.

Laura Nesbitt – Open Water Swimmer. Open Water Swim Coach. Really good at both. Vastly experienced and dedicated club coach with a deep respect for the virtues of hard work and training, and a strong desire to encourage youth participation. She has produced a whole raft of regional and national qualifiers and medallists, both in the pool and open water. I needed someone who squeals with excitement at sea conditions which send most people home. Laura is a master of the technical skills required to swim well, but also of the less definable skills that help to combat the conspiratory partnership of unforgiving sea, unpredictable physical response and fickle human emotion. Laura is my boss on the day of the swim because she knows my swimming; happy to accompany me for a couple of hours of cold, windy training in the lake and sea. She is adept at telling me what I'm doing wrong and how to fix it. One day, maybe, she might also tell me if I'm doing something right.

Paul Wells – Skipper of Ruby D, has been fishing and sailing these waters for decades. He's got the boat, the charts, the satellite navigation kit, the echo sounder, but most of all a vast wealth of knowledge from working with this stretch of the channel. He piloted Jo for his crossing and was enthusiastic from my first moment of contacting him. It was Paul's agreement to skipper me across, followed by his swiftly compiled menu of possible dates that kickstarted the whole process. Meeting Paul on Ruby D at Portishead Marina, absorbing the size of the boat, seeing the ladder, sink, kettle, loo and chart table; listening to him wax knowledgeably about the channel as he pointed at the charts; suddenly I felt like I was ready to announce my intentions to others.

Gavin Oliver – Swiss Army Knife in human form. Resourceful, enthusiastic, energetic, upbeat and reliable. Off the plane from Croatia at 9:00pm, on the boat in Portishead by 5:00am. Gav slotted into the crew in place of Jo with only two days' notice. He has swum with me in all sorts of places, conditions and temperatures and listened to me perpetually

153

bang on about my training, feeding regime, fears and foibles. He was probably eager to make sure I completed the swim, so he wouldn't have to take the ear-bashing any longer. Take a Gav with you on every adventure.

Jake Richardson – The eldest of my three boys. Just turned eighteen but already an adventurer at heart. Has cycled Lon Las Cymru with me and provided kayak support for my Swanage Pier to Studland Beach swim last year. We've had plenty of other adventures with Stan and Eddie too and I'm thrilled at what a great role model he has become for his brothers. He was coming along for the adventure, to take a few photographs and to manage the social media updates. Our last summer before university so, most of all, he was there to leap in and do the last bit of the swim with me.

Joanna Richardson – Land Support and in it for the long haul. It is pretty much impossible to thank Jo enough for her support. She has been there since long before I filled my time with this swimming lark. She endured the decade of me being far less of a man than I should have been, and now has to suffer my attempts to make up that ground, no matter how ridiculous the ideas are. She is inherently a worrier; sees stress and peril where the rest of us see fun and excitement. It can be an intense worry, and is rarely eased with logic and rationality. I do not say this to complain, I am acknowledging it, in the hope that she believes me when I say that I understand the fretfulness of my antics. I am sure she wishes I would just throw my energy into getting promoted or redecorating the house: anything but go and test myself in an environment she finds fearful. Jo does not share the same love for the water as me and our three boys. I do not go through these things as a confident man, doubts are with me most of the way and she is my sounding board, gently pointing me back on course, keeping me ticking over. I couldn't do any of this without her.

Appendix B - BOAT TRACKER DATA

PENARTH TO CLEVEDON SWIM

15 minute interval positions

Time(clock)	Time(hrs)	Lat. DMS	Lon. DMS	OS Grid Ref
6:30:00	0.00	51° 26' 10.4958"	-3° 10' 0.9804"	ST 18982 71451
6:45:47	0.25	51° 25' 51.006"	-3° 9' 33.0732"	ST 19511 70841
7:00:47	0.50	51° 25' 24.6174"	-3° 9' 20.9766"	ST 19732 70022
7:15:47	0.75	51° 25' 0.3714"	-3° 9' 0.576"	ST 20114 69267
7:30:47	1.00	51° 24' 44.2722"	-3° 8' 35.6346"	ST 20588 68762
7:45:47	1.25	51° 24' 32.742"	-3° 8' 2.292"	ST 21226 68396
8:00:47	1.50	51° 24' 32.0616"	-3° 7' 23.4078"	ST 21977 68363
8:15:47	1.75	51° 24' 36.1506"	-3° 6' 40.7844"	ST 22803 68477
8:30:47	2.00	51° 24' 35.319"	-3° 5' 53.541"	ST 23715 68437
8:45:47	2.25	51° 24' 40.392"	-3° 4' 53.0364"	ST 24886 68577
9:00:47	2.50	51° 24' 53.1102"	-3° 3' 46.623"	ST 26175 68951
9:15:47	2.75	51° 25' 1.7538"	-3° 2' 43.2234	ST 27403 69200
9:30:47	3.00	51° 25' 23.1306"	-3° 1' 56.0496"	ST 28324 69848
9:45:47	3.25	51° 25' 41.1234"	-3° 1' 11.3694"	ST 29195 70391
10:00:47	3.50	51° 26' 2.1804"	-3° 0' 23.9106"	ST 30120 71029
10:15:47	3.75	51° 26' 22.2462"	-2° 59' 16.6482"	ST 31427 71631
10:30:47	4.00	51° 26' 32.085"	-2° 58' 23.124"	ST 32465 71921
10:45:47	4.25	51° 26' 37.8162"	-2° 57' 28.1124"	ST 33529 72085
11:00:47	4.50	51° 26' 40.6896"	-2° 56' 34.08"	ST 34573 72160
11:15:47	4.75	51° 26' 41.928"	-2° 55' 31.782"	ST 35776 72183
11:30:47	5.00	51° 26' 41.7552"	-2° 54' 34.5954"	ST 36880 72163
11:45:47	5.25	51° 26' 41.5278"	-2° 53' 42.6192"	ST 37884 72144
12:00:47	5.50	51° 26' 36.7866"	-2° 53' 0.4848"	ST 38695 71988
12:15:47	5.75	51° 26' 35.3574"	-2° 52' 15.207"	ST 39569 71933
12:28:00	5.97	51° 26' 30.66"	-2° 51' 43.0914	ST 40187 71781

Appendix C - TRAINING SWIM RECORDS

6 Mile Training Swim – Alec Richardson
Sunday 9th July 7am, Clevedon Lake

Water Temp: 21 deg

Conditions: Very calm, slight breeze in last hour. Sunny with light cloud.

Mile 1:   28:41
Mile 2:   29:28
Mile 3:   29:24
Mile 4:   30:02
Mile 5:   31:00
Mile 6:   31:58

Feeds:

- Maltodextrin mix (50g maltodextrin per 100ml) – similar to Maxim
- Bananas
- Soft dried apricots
- Warm, sweet tea

(Fed between each mile)

30 mins: 200ml Water

60 mins: 100g (200ml) Maltodextrin, 100ml Water, small banana

90 mins: 100g (200ml) Maltodextrin, 100ml Water

120 mins: 100g (200ml) Maltodextrin, 100ml Water, 4 apricots, 100ml warm tea

150 mins: 100g (200ml) Maltodextrin, 100ml Water

180 mins: 100g (200ml) Maltodextrin, 200ml Water, 200ml warm tea, Aldi fruit/nut bar

NOTES:

Got out to do feeds and took longer over them than would do in actual swim.

Water a bit warm.

No issues with maltodextrin mix during swim, but caused a few bowel issues about 2 hours after swim (would this therefore happen during 6 hour swim?)

Feel like I would prefer more solid intake – boiled eggs, crustless peanut butter/honey sandwiches?

Hat slipping up off ears during last hour.

Slowing (as per times) but still felt in control of stroke and no significant pain.

8 Mile Training Swim – Alec Richardson

Sunday 16th July 7am, Clevedon Lake

Water Temp: 18 deg

Conditions: Very calm, slight breeze in last hour. Grey cloud, air temp 18 deg.

Mile 1: 29:04
Mile 2: 28:57
Mile 3: 29:52
Mile 4: 30:13
Mile 5: 30:54
Mile 6: 32:16
Mile 7: 32:46
Mile 8: 33:40

Feeds:

- Maltodextrin/Dextrose mix (50g maltodextrin/50g dextrose per 300ml) – similar to Maxim
- Bananas
- Hard Boiled Eggs
- Ground Porridge oats mixed with water and honey (50g oats per 250ml)
- Warm, sweet tea

(Fed between each mile)

30 mins: 300ml Water
60 mins: 80g (250ml) Malto/dextro, 150ml Water, half banana
90 mins: 80g (250ml) Malto/dextro, 150ml Water
120 mins: 80g (250ml) Malto/dextro, 150ml Water, half boiled egg
150 mins: 80g (250ml) Malto/dextro, 100ml Warm tea
180 mins: ~~80g (250ml) Malto/dextro~~ (not taken), 200ml Porridge/Honey mix
210 mins: 80g (250ml) Malto/dextro, 100ml Warm tea
240 mins: 80g (250ml) Malto/dextro, 200ml Water, half boiled egg, 200ml warm tea

NOTES:

Got out to do feeds and took longer over them than would do in actual swim.

Water and air a bit cooler than last big swim, but still warmer than likely channel temp.

No issues with malto/dextro mix during swim, but did miss out 180 min dose as felt quite bloated. Missed two planned water doses as felt like I had no room for it.

Porridge/honey mix was very settling – incorporate more? Boiled eggs also good – not pleasant to eat, but good in stomach.

Still need to try crustless peanut butter/honey sandwiches?

Orange hat not slipping as much as blue did last week.

Slowing (as per times) but still felt in control of stroke and no significant pain.

Appendix D - ANTICIPATED SWIM SPEED

Alec Richardson, July 2017
Based on 6 and 8 mile lake swims. Good, flat conditions.
Data for Penarth to Clevedon Swim

HOUR	DISTANCE per HOUR (m)	With 2 x 1min feed stops
1	3300	3200
2	3200	3100
3	3050	2950
4	2900	2800
5	2750	2650
6	2600	2500
7	2450	2350
8	2350	2250

Appendix E - FEED SCHEDULES

PLANNED SCHEDULE

INTERVAL	TIME	PROPOSED FEED	ACTUAL FEED
0 hr 30		250 ml Water	
1 hr		250 ml (80g) Maldex 100 ml Water Half Boiled Egg	
1 hr 30		250 ml (80g) Maldex 100 ml Water	
2 hr		250 ml Oat Smoothie 100 ml Water	
2 hr 30		250 ml (80g) Maldex 150 ml Warm Tea	
3 hr		250 ml (80g) Maldex 100 ml Water Half Boiled Egg	(IBUPROFEN)
3 hr 30		250 ml (80g) Maldex 150 ml Warm Tea	
4 hr		250 ml Oat Smoothie 100 ml Water	(ELECTROLYTES)
4 hr 30		250 ml (80g) Maldex 100 ml Water 3 x Jelly Babies	
5 hr		250 ml (80g) Maldex 100 ml Water Half Boiled Egg	
5 hr 30		250 ml (80g) Maldex 150 ml Warm Tea	
6 hr		250 ml Oat Smoothie 100 ml Water	
6 hr 30		250 ml (80g) Maldex 100 ml Water	
7 hr		250 ml (80g) Maldex 100 ml Water Half Boiled Egg	
7 hr 30		250 ml (80g) Maldex 150 ml Warm Tea	
8 hr		250 ml Oat Smoothie 100 ml Water 3 x Jelly Babies	

ACTUAL FEED RECORD FROM SWIM

INTERVAL	TIME	PROPOSED FEED	STROKES (per min)	FEED TIME (min, sec)
0 hr	6:30 am		62	
0 hr 30	7:00 am	250 ml Water	61	0' 43"
1 hr	7:30 am	250 ml (80g) Maldex ~~100 ml Water~~ (not taken) Half Boiled Egg	58	2' 32"
1 hr 30	8:00 am	250 ml (80g) Maldex ~~100~~ 50 ml Water	57	1' 20"
2 hr	8:30 am	250 ml Oat Smoothie (not finished) 100 ml Water (not finished)	62 (59 on the 15 minute) Between Monkton Rock and Flat Holm	1' 27"
2 hr 30	9:00 am	250 ml (80g) Maldex 150 ml Warm Tea	60 (58 on the 15 minute)	1' 35"
3 hr	9:30 am	250 ml (80g) Maldex 100 ml Water Half Boiled Egg (IBUPROFEN)	59	2' 32"
3 hr 30	10:00 am	250 ml (80g) Maldex 150 ml Warm Tea	56 (57 on the 15 minute – critical point)	1' 40"
4 hr	10:30 am	250 ml Oat Smoothie ~~100 ml Water~~ (not taken) (ELECTROLYTES)	56 (52 on the 15 minute)	2' 55"
4 hr 30	11:00 am	250 ml (80g) Maldex 100 ml Water (swig) ~~3~~ 4 x Jelly Babies (spat out)	56	2' 00"
5 hr	11:30 am	250 ml (80g) Maldex ~~100 ml Water~~ (not taken) ~~Half Boiled Egg~~ (not taken)	60	1' 32"
5 hr 30	12:00 pm	~~250 ml (80g) Maldex~~ ~~150 ml Warm Tea~~	59 Did not feed	N/A
< 6 hr	< 12:30 pm	~~250 ml Oat Smoothie~~ ~~100 ml Water~~	52 Did not feed	N/A

161

NOTES ON FEEDS:

My feed times were longer than anticipated. Partly as I hadn't accounted for how long it would take me to stop swimming, approach the boat and then position myself to reach the basket. Partly the roughness of the water just making me cautious about swallowing and trying not to spill everything into the sea.

At 3 hr 30, Laura notes 'critical point' - this is when trying to break through the strongest flow in the shipping lane, so needing to keep my output high, but also in the roughest section where my stroke rate dropped as I attempted to work with the wave timings.

Appendix F - KIT LIST *(ANNOTATED)*

Penarth to Clevedon Swim
Alec Richardson 2017

Swim Kit

    Trunks *worked fine – not used since*

    Goggles, 3 pairs, clear, tinted and polarised *polarised were good for whole swim*

    Ear plugs + spares silicone 'putty' *stayed in place for whole swim and came out ok at end*

    Hat + spares *orange 'Clevedon Pier' Nancy Farmer designed hat stayed put for whole swim*

    Waterproof sunscreen (Riemann P20) *brilliant – apply properly, best I've found*

    Rubber Gloves (for greasing up) *thin latex ones – useful and look good too*

    Vaseline *actually bargain shop unbranded petroleum jelly – worked great*

Drugs

    Ibuprofen tablets *took after 3 hours prophylactically based on 8 mile training swim*

    Anti-histamine (non-drowsy, for jellyfish stings) *not needed*

    Sea sickness tablets (never needed before, but Jake may also need them on the boat) *not needed*

    Sudocrem *not needed*

General Kit

    Binoculars *made it more interesting for crew – lots to look at in Bristol Channel*

    Small whiteboards and pens *heavily used – great for communicating messages as I fed*

    Stopwatches (for timing swim and stroke count/pace) *used – three for official timing*

    Clothes pegs *I didn't need them – used by crew to stop bin bags blowing away etc.?*

    Black bin bags for rubbish *used*

    Wet wipes for hands *yes, always useful, take them everywhere!*

Warm clothes   *crew needed them – I would have needed them if I'd abandoned*

Waterproof   *great to throw on once changed to keep spray off without being too hot*

Large Towels + changing robe   *again – would have been useful if I'd abandoned*

Clipboard, pens, copy of feed schedule to record feed and stroke rate   *useful*

Duct tape   *not needed, but you never know……..*

Copy of BLDSA swim recognition form   *essential for observer (Steve) to record conditions etc.*

Feed (Pre-mixed) + Schedule

(all worked well, plenty left over)

Bottles of Maldex mixture
Bottles of Oat/honey/banana smoothie
Bottles of water
Bottles for tea
Boiled Eggs
5-litre flask of hot water + bungees to secure it
Teabags, milk and sachets of hot chocolate and sugar
Bananas, cereal bars, jelly babies and a couple of energy gels   *not needed as didn't abandon*
Food for crew   *they all agreed to sort themselves out*

Equipment to feed
Pole and basket   *worked well throughout*
Kayakers emergency throw line (as back up if feed pole breaks/gets lost overboard)   *not needed*
Spare drinks bottles   *not needed*
Spare energy powders, bottles of water etc.   *not needed*
Prototype feed basket (in case new one breaks or gets lost)   *not needed*

Communication and Media

    Smartphone for social media updates (Jake, Gavin and Laura) *excellent, really added something*

    Action-cam (Laura) *good, apart from Laura capturing me vassing-up in latex gloves*

    Camera (Jake) *great – really nice to see how it all looked from the boat*

    GPS Tracker (on boat – Jake) *fantastic to have data to look back on*

After Swim – On beach with Jo (NOT ON BOAT!)

    Towels *useful*

    Quick-Dri Tracksuit *love this - essential to cover up quickly in front of cameras*

    Clothes and shoes *a real feeling of returning to normality to pull on shorts and t-shirt*

    Chicken salad sandwich *solid food – best sandwich ever, ever….. ever!*

    Snacks *yup, good*

    Flask of tea *have not yet discovered words joyful enough for this*

Appendix G – CHARITY?

So many people asked (understandably) if I was doing the swim to raise money for a particular cause. I wasn't. I have done plenty of that over the past few years, with compelling reason, but not this time.

The social media post below was my answer to this question.

CHARITY?

I am not doing this for a particular cause or charity, but many people have said they would happily contribute if I were.

If my swim inspires you in any way to do something, then I have three suggestions:

1. MARLENS. This is the charity which maintains Clevedon Marine Lake. They secured huge funding to refurbish the lake and it is now a busy and valuable part of the community. Consider a small financial donation via their website, or if you have time to volunteer then let them know via their facebook page.

2. Relatives and close friends of my family have been, and continue to be, affected by cancer in many devastating ways over the past few years but I have been honoured to see immense strength and resilience in the face of such an unfair and uncompromising illness. There are people I will have at the forefront of my mind during the swim to remind me there are much tougher challenges than a few miles of water. You choose - a hospice, a research organisation, a charity shop - just consider giving a little bit of time or money.

3. Everyone is fighting a battle of some sort. I know many of us use open water swimming (and the social contact it brings)

as therapy one way or another. Perhaps use your enthusiasm for whatever you love doing to encourage someone else to try it. Have a chat with a stranger. Offer the bus driver a bite of your kebab....... you get the idea.......

Appendix H – A WELCOME MESSAGE

This is the email I received from Mark Finch (mentioned way back in the text somewhere) after completing the swim. I don't include it to be smug, but because he is someone I have always thought of as an adventurous soul. I was just simply thrilled to hear that he approved of me setting my sights on something local.

Hi Alec,

Congratulations! What an amazing achievement - and in under 6 hours, too! Presumably you arrived on the beach at Clevedon just about 24 hours after we saw you swimming round to Ladye Bay on Tuesday.

Of all the fantastic things that teachers at (our school) get up to in their own time, this is just about the best thing I've heard about. What I really admire is that what you've done is right on our doorstep - there's no carbon footprint. It's just a celebration of who you are, where you are and when you are. Well done that man!

Regards,

Mark

Appendix I – BLACKADDER MOMENTS

I wrote this a couple of years before this swim, before it was even on my radar, but I think it demonstrates that the Bristol Channel had already become an important part of my life. I thought I'd have a go at getting my thoughts down after reading "I Love Open Water Swimming" pieces from other readers in the back of H2Open magazine (now Outdoor Swimmer) – sent it in on a whim, and they published it (slightly shortened) in the very next issue!

BLACKADDER MOMENTS

I love Open Water Swimming, and I know I do because it always takes me back to the joy of TV comedy of my youth.

I loved Black Adder. It was unquestionably funny and a hugely influential part of my formative years. I don't remember all the funny bits and I'm not entirely sure I could justify why I enjoyed it so much but many years later I still know for certain that I loved it.

In the 1980's if you wanted to watch something on TV, you had to wait for it to be broadcast, sit down, watch it and really concentrate - for the entire time it was on. No series record, no pause and rewind, no streaming, downloads or box-sets. Be there to watch it, or miss out. Yes, we had a VCR but that primitive technology was not to be relied upon for something this important.

Black Adder was prioritised over everything, nothing got in the way. I saw every episode of the first two series at their first showing. I enjoyed looking in the Radio Times to check the schedule and the anticipation grew exponentially throughout the week. Every episode rewarded my patience admirably and I was left feeling that it had all been worth the wait.

I really miss those days of nurturing reward from a patient life. I could fill this page bemoaning our modern world of instant gratification in which waiting is becoming an obsolete concept, but perhaps I should move on to why I love Open Water Swimming.

Along with a surprising number of wonderful and interesting people I do most of my swimming at Clevedon in the Severn Estuary. This is an uncompromising stretch of water. It has a tidal range of about 12 metres. An hour either side of high water it flows faster than any of us can swim. It is brown and silty; underwater visibility is six inches at best. We all emerge from the water bearded, regardless of gender. It's hard to say what lurks in the depths, but we sometimes get bumped from below and the local fisherman often hook out some sizeable congers. There are limited places and infrequent, narrow windows of time in which you can enter and exit the water; get it wrong and you're stuck waist deep in mud watching the incoming tide rush to greet you.

You don't swim in the water here when you feel like it; you swim when, and only when, it lets you. If you want to swim here you have to patiently gain knowledge and respectfully heed the wisdom of those who've spent years doing it before you. You have to acquire skills. If you would like to increase your opportunities for swimming then you'd better learn how to cope with rough water and how to swim in the dark. You need a basic understanding of relative velocity and be able to quickly gauge your movement against landmarks, recognising when and how to work with the flow. There will be constant, awkward negotiations with your family as the tide pays no heed to your finely crafted domestic routines. If you want to swim for longer in the cold of the winter you had better have put in the months of effort to acclimatise. There are no short-cuts, no magic bits of modern electronic kit or downloadable 'apps' to help you swim more and shiver less, only your own patient effort. Read all the 'expert' blogs if you like, but don't expect that to be a substitute for gaining experience in the water. If you want to swim here, you really have to love your swimming. You can, however, be absolutely certain that any company you have for your swim feels the same way about it as you do.

Much like hunting Black Adder episodes among the pages of the Radio Times, a careful scouring of my little yellow tide tables reveals a couple of Sundays every year when high water, sunset, moonrise and friends just happen to align. The anticipation of these swimming episodes obliterates the usual dread of Monday morning. The calendar ticks over, the evening arrives and friends gather. Hobble off the pebbled beach to swim under the pier with the flow. A mile up the coast turn with the tide and start the journey back. Be sure to do some proper head-up breaststroke to watch the sun set below the pier. As it gets close to dropping off the edge of the world marvel at how the surface of the water seems oddly blue. Concentrate, don't miss a moment, there's no rewind button. Roll back onto the beach, twist the top off the flask and gratefully accept a slice of something home-baked from a reassuringly familiar silhouette against the darkening sky.

In my mid-innings years, as the world accelerates away from me, these are my Black Adder moments and I have invested time and effort to make them possible. This is how I know I love open water swimming.

Alec Richardson

13033056R00106

Printed in Great Britain
by Amazon